Being
with
Busyness

Being
with
Busyness

Zen Ways
to Transform
Overwhelm
and Burnout

Brother Phap Huu and Jo Confino

Cohosts of the Plum Village podcast *The Way Out Is In*

PARALLAX PRESS
BERKELEY, CALIFORNIA

Parallax Press
2236B Sixth Street
Berkeley, CA 94710
parallax.org

Parallax Press is the publishing division of
Plum Village Community of Engaged Buddhism, Inc.
© 2024 Plum Village Community of
Engaged Buddhism and Jo Confino
All rights reserved

Cover art by Brother Phap Huu
Cover design by Katie Eberle
Text design by Maureen Forys, Happenstance Type-O-Rama
Author photograph courtesy of Jo Confino

Printed in the United States of America by Versa Press
Printed on FSC paper

ISBN 978-1-952692-87-1 | Ebook ISBN 978-1-952692-88-8
LCCN: 2024035057

1 2 3 4 5 Versa 28 27 26 25 24

Life waits patiently for true heroes. It is dangerous when those aspiring to be heroes cannot wait until they find themselves. When aspiring heroes have not found themselves, they are tempted to borrow the world's weapons—money, fame, and power—to fight their battles.

These weapons cannot protect the inner life of the hero. To cope with fears and insecurities, the premature hero has to stay busy all the time. The destructive capacity of nonstop busyness rivals nuclear weapons and is as addictive as opium. It empties the life of the spirit. False heroes find it easier to make war than deal with the emptiness in their own souls.

Thich Nhat Hanh, *Fragrant Palm Leaves*

Contents

Welcome   xi

PART 1   Busyness, Overwhelm, and Burnout

The Buddha Also Suffered   6

No Mud, No Lotus   8

Busyness in Plum Village   13

Feeling Overwhelm in the Body   15

Practice: Smiling to Our Overwhelm   17

Embracing Our Overwhelm   20

Knowing Our Capacity and Learning

   When to Stop   22

A Bell of Mindfulness   25

Allow Yourself Space to Do Nothing   27

Develop a Practice before Life Gets Difficult   30

Our Work Points in the Direction of Our

   Inner Healing   32

Can't Change the System with the Same

   Thinking That Created the Mess   35

Walk in Freedom   37

Practice: Walking on the Earth   39

Coming Home   42

The Power of Humility   45

Taking Care of the Fire Within   49

Simple Commitments Can Change

    the World   52

Eco-Anxiety and Taking Refuge

    in the Earth   56

Practice: The Five Remembrances   58

The Spaciousness of Silence   60

The Power of Presence   64

Get Real: Bringing Presence to

    Difficult Conversations   67

Collective Transformation   70

Vulnerability Is the Opening to Possibility   72

The Island of the Self   78

Pain and Poetry: A Zen Master's Example   81

The New Way Is the Ancient Way:

    Ripening, Reciprocity, and Regeneration   87

Letting Go of the Need to Be in Control   92

Real Community and Belonging   94

Impermanence   97

Practice: Stop and Lay Down

    Your Burdens   100

PART 2 Healthy Boundaries

Two Faces of Compassion   106

Saying No Is a Mantra   109

Bitter Melon Soup   112

Courageous Communication   116

Transforming Toxic Feedback with a
    Mirror of Mindfulness   119

Protecting Ourselves from Toxicity
    and Abuse   121

The Attack-Back Syndrome   126

Beginning Anew   129

Practice: Beginning Anew   131

A Bell of Mindfulness in Meetings   134

Digging Two Graves   138

The Art of Letting Go   140

Never Too Late to Make Peace   143

Interbeing, No-Self, and Boundaries   145

From a Murderer to a Monk   149

Don't Let Boundaries Become Barriers   152

Boundaries Create Space for Our
    Deeper Aspirations to Manifest   154

Making Mistakes Is a Way to Grow   158

Your Presence Changes the World   161

Dharma Rain   163

*Practice: Offering Strength and Space
    to Loved Ones*   164

Appreciation   167

References   169

About the Authors   171

About *The Way Out Is In* Podcast   175

Welcome

Hello dear friends! We are Brother Phap Huu and Jo Confino. We've been walking alongside each other on the spiritual path for eighteen years, and we cohost the podcast *The Way Out Is In*. We've written this book together in the spirit of friendship, with a very clear purpose: to offer balm for the modern ailment of busyness that so many of us are experiencing.

In this book, we draw on our own life experiences and the collective wisdom of Zen practitioners throughout time. We share practices that have helped shape our own lives, which we hope will offer you practical support at times when you develop that tightening in your body and mind—signs that you are stressed from doing too much and feeling there is too little time.

But first, let us introduce ourselves.

BROTHER PHAP HUU: I'm Brother Phap Huu, the abbot of Plum Village's Upper Hamlet monastery in southwest France, a position that Zen Master Thich Nhat Hanh, or Thay as he is known, asked me to take on at the tender age of twenty-four. As abbot, it is my role to look after the well-being of a hundred monastic and lay residents as well as thousands of visitors each year. I ordained as a Zen Buddhist monk at the age of fourteen and was the personal attendant of Thay (which means teacher in Vietnamese) for fifteen years. So, even though I was accustomed to managing responsibilities as Thay's attendant and later as vice-abbot for three years, you can imagine that when I became the abbot of one of Europe's largest Buddhist monasteries, I quickly learned what it feels like to be overwhelmed! And yes, despite being well practiced in the art and science of mindfulness, we monastics do also face burnout.

JO CONFINO: I'm Jo Confino, working at the intersection of personal transformation and systems change as a leadership coach and spiritual mentor for activists and leaders in the climate movement, business, and the arts. Like Brother Phap Huu, I've had periods of overwhelm, particularly in my forty-year career as a journalist, during which I faced tough deadlines, complex editorial decisions, and difficult ethical choices. I have also known times best characterized by the English phrase "when it rains, it pours," meaning that difficult situations sometimes follow each other in rapid succession or happen all at once. One moment my life has appeared to be in relative balance, and the next, it has felt like it was falling apart.

Thay's calligraphy "The Way Out Is In" is the subject of our deep contemplation for this book as well as for the podcast series we cocreate and cohost. This phrase encapsulates the core healing journey of our lives: the way out of suffering starts with looking inside and gaining insights before putting them into practice in order to help transform our situation and find a deeper sense of well-being and happiness.

PART 1

Busyness, Overwhelm, and Burnout

Many of us are leading busy, complex lives, caught in a vortex of needs, wishes, plans, tasks, and projects. Each of us in our own way works hard to juggle competing needs for our attention, but on occasion things can spiral out of control, leading to feelings of overwhelm and even burnout. It's like the spinning plates act at the circus. There are only so many spinning plates the entertainer can keep in balance on their poles before some start to crash to the ground.

Our "busyness" is never only ours. In the light of *interbeing*, a word Thich Nhat Hanh coined to show that nothing can exist by itself alone, we can see that by taking too much on, we cannot help but make others busy; in turn, others' busyness ripples out and puts us under greater pressure. It is a collective societal issue caused, in part, by the demands of the capitalist system in which many of us live, a system that values striving and individualism and often generates the belief that we are not good enough and therefore have to achieve even more.

When we become overwhelmed, we can quickly lose our ability to respond effectively to our situation and we may have the sense of wanting to escape or to stay in bed, curl up in a ball, and pull the blankets over our head. We may experience depression, anger, anxiety, or numbness. Anyone can feel overwhelmed, regardless of their age, class, race, or gender.

In our daily work, the two of us are privileged to listen to a wide range of people whose lives are interconnected with our own: leaders, teachers, activists, corporate executives, spiritual seekers, as well as our friends and family members. We have found no one who is immune to this feeling of sometimes being engulfed by life.

That is why we gave this book the title *Being with Busyness*—we recognize that we cannot escape our many individual and collective responsibilities. We need to earn a living, nurture our families and friends, and deal with the many other demands of daily life, whether it be our health or taxes. We are also collectively confronting the poly-crisis of climate change, uncontrolled pollution, and ecosystem collapse, spurred on by our insatiable appetites and our focus on consumption and extraction, all of which threaten the very existence of our civilization and endangers the natural world. As if this were not enough, we are also facing the tyranny of technologies that bring all the world to our doorstep all the time.

In this era, when so much stress and anxiety are filling our hearts and minds, how can we embrace joy and a sense of ease? There is a growing recognition that one effective response is to look back to the ancient wisdom of our ancestors for guidance and support rather than to continue to thrust ever forward. Buddhist teachings are more than 2,600 years old and are as relevant today as the moment the Buddha started sharing the fruits of his enlightenment sitting under the Bodhi tree. We both feel very lucky and privileged that the causes and conditions in our lives, albeit in very different ways, have brought us into the presence of a modern Zen master such as Thay and the mindfulness practices of the Plum Village lineage of Buddhism that he and his students have established over the past seventy years.

Not only did Thay develop a profound understanding of Buddhist teachings but more importantly, he integrated them so deeply into his way of being that he had an extraordinary capacity to synthesize the teachings of the Buddha and transmit them to others in the most simple, accessible, and yet profound way. That kind of integration is perhaps the clearest example of the quality of pure presence, which Thay exuded in abundance.

In this book, we seek to continue this approach, reflecting on some core insights of Buddhism and making them relevant to today's world and to our everyday experiences. By integrating some of these insights into your life, you will be able to recognize the early signs of overwhelm and burnout and begin to transform whatever situation you are facing in order to come back home to yourself and into a greater sense of balance. In doing so, you not only benefit yourself, but also all the people around you, your family, friends, colleagues, and society. Just as your busyness is contagious, so is your more peaceful presence.

Busyness, overwhelm, and even burnout are ultimately not problems for us to solve using force—if we see them in this way, we may well end up suffering from the overwhelm of trying to make the feeling of overwhelm go away! Instead, if we can have insight into our suffering and learn to understand and befriend our emotions and see them as our teachers, they will be sure to point us in the direction of home, to our inherent peaceful nature.

The Buddha Also Suffered

It may be comforting to remember that even enlightened people suffer. While we might imagine the Buddha as a god-like figure, we have to remember he was a human being who faced immense challenges in his life. Thich Nhat Hanh also had to deal with intense difficulties, especially during the war in Vietnam, which on occasion overwhelmed him. Our insights and practices are born from carving a path through our own pain, not out of intellectual curiosity or the development of concepts or ideas. That is why we can place some faith in the guidance of people who have walked before us and know that it works.

Thay wrote a letter to his monastic students shortly before his stroke in 2014, in which he shared the many difficulties the Buddha had encountered. Referring to himself in the third person as was traditional among elders of his generation, he reframes suffering as pointing to a Dharma door, an opening in life that allows us to access the truth of existence.

> The Sangha [community] of the Buddha and the
> Buddha himself suffered division, defamation,

and the Buddha was almost assassinated more than once. In the last years of his life, the Buddha had to witness the destruction of his homeland by an evil king.... Of course, the Buddha practiced to handle his suffering by using his understanding and compassion. We are the same. In the past, Thay did not know the practice and so allowed himself to be overwhelmed by suffering and jealousy. Trickery and discrimination brought him so much resentment, disappointment, and even despair. Fortunately, this suffering was what motivated Thay to look for suitable Dharma doors to practice and the merit of his ancestors helped him to find them.

We too can be motivated by our suffering to look for ways out of it. We're lucky to have come across a path that practitioners have followed for millennia.

No Mud, No Lotus

JO CONFINO: The core of the Buddha's teachings is the Four Noble Truths. The first truth is to acknowledge the presence of suffering and the second is to recognize the causes of suffering. Thay was very clear that our busyness is often the result of our inability to face and acknowledge the underlying suffering that may exist beneath the surface of our lives.

"People try to cover up their suffering by being busy," he told me. "Maybe it is not because they like to be busy, but they want to get busy in order not to have the time to touch the suffering in themselves." This statement is profound. He talked of the importance of helping people "realize the suffering is there, and that there is a way to take care of their suffering."

"If we are skillful enough," he continued, "we will help them to stop being busy, take the time to come back and take care of themselves, and then they can take care of the Earth."

So, before we start looking for pathways to healing, it's important to begin by recognizing and understanding the challenges we face individually and collectively.

In the hearts of the many people I coach, I find a near-universal, profound wish to come home, to belong, to be free. What this points to is an experience of life right now that feels the opposite: people feel dispersed and trapped by their responsibilities, and they have lost their connection to what is most important to them and their sense of peace and joy in life.

Many of us experience being pulled in a thousand directions, forced into multitasking in a way that makes it difficult to devote time and focus to any one aspect of our lives. Multitasking increases our stress hormone cortisol as well as adrenaline, the fight-or-flight hormone. As a result of trying to keep the wheels on the bus going, we don't feel able to slow down or rest—we are often running on empty. Does this sound familiar?

This experience of disenchantment and alienation can have the perverse effect of making people strive even harder. We often believe that we will find the answer outside of ourselves, often in our external achievements. "If only I can get over this next hurdle, then everything will be OK," we promise ourselves as we struggle with the next deadline, crisis, or must-do item on our agenda.

Often the result is that we can't find the bandwidth to focus our attention on what is most important in our lives. When we take the time to step back from our everyday lives by practicing mindfulness or taking a retreat, insights about the deepest parts of our lives tend to rise up naturally. At a recent activists' retreat in Plum Village, one woman shared that she realized in a very concrete way that she was causing her children to suffer. After a hard day's work, she saw that her mind was still focused on her many projects and to-do lists even while sitting at the dinner table with her children. This was making them feel neglected and unseen. From that moment, she made a vow to do her best to give them her full attention whenever she was with them and to put healthier boundaries in place between her work and her family. Another retreatant, working in the field of climate change, said that she was so busy trying to save the world's forests from destruction that she had not yet found the time to take her own child to explore the beauty and majesty of the woodlands near her home.

Beyond the busyness of everyday life, we must factor in the powerful attraction of social media and other countless, close-at-hand opportunities to distract our minds from real issues. While seeking entertainment or pleasure is natural and can temporarily alleviate feelings of overwhelm, when we use these distractions to avoid our suffering, they actually end up adding to our stress because, whether we like it or not, we always end up having to come back and face reality.

In my coaching practice, I observe that people often feel lonely in their overwhelm, even when they know intellectually that it is an increasingly common ailment.

Our collective obsession with showing our best face to the world, especially on social media, means difficulties are often airbrushed away, and we don't feel able to share openly for fear of being seen as a failure. When clients are able to look above the parapet and recognize that their experience is part of a collective malaise, they breathe a huge sigh of relief.

The truth is that we are living in unprecedented times. Beyond our own personal lives, we are constantly inundated with the woes of the world through 24/7 news and social media. The climate emergency, the collapse of biodiversity, increasing global inequality and conflict, and the rise of extremism and misinformation have come together in a perfect storm. This poly-crisis is generating anxiety, grief, and even despair, thereby adding to already-present feelings of overwhelm and powerlessness.

Thus we see clearly the First and Second Noble Truths: suffering exists, and its presence is caused by specific conditions. The good news is that the Buddha identified the Third and Fourth Noble Truths, namely that suffering can be transformed, and there is a path leading to the cessation of suffering. This book offers ways to recognize the difficult truths of our times and simultaneouslye generate what Joanna Macy, the eco-philosopher and Buddhist scholar, refers to as "active hope." Thay's saying "no mud, no lotus," helps us to understand that the suffering in our life is like the mud that provides the nourishment for a beautiful lotus flower to bloom. So, rather than turning away from our pain, or denying that it even exists, we can transform our understanding and recognize our experience of suffering as a key ingredient in generating pathways to our individual and collective happiness. If we take our suffering away, we also take away our opportunity for happiness.

Busyness in Plum Village

BROTHER PHAP HUU: Some people have the idea that as monastics, we are always calm, relaxed, and sitting in meditation, but the truth is that our life is very dynamic and at times we are tremendously busy. We receive thousands of guests every year in Plum Village on retreat, and we also hold specialized retreats for groups of scientists, climate activists, ecologists, business leaders, young meditation practitioners, and families with children. Plum Village is one of the few Zen meditation centers that welcomes families with children and teenagers, and holding programs for them all summer takes a lot of energy to manage. We don't have paid employees who organize and run our retreats; instead, the retreats are staffed by monks and nuns with the support of lay volunteers. We welcome retreatants into our home—Plum Village is where we live—so even during rest periods, we don't get very much rest! There are also the many trips we take to bring the Dharma to communities all over the world, and each of these takes an enormous amount of organizing. On top of all that, we must take care of the three practice centers we have here in southwest France—one for the monks and two for the nuns.

So, we are busy, but our busyness also has elements of Zen practice: there are the nourishing elements of joy and play, and we have a lot of fun on these retreats. There is also the element of study, because we continually learn from the human engagement that comes from welcoming people into our monastery. Coming to Plum Village is a deep dive inward—not just for the visiting practitioners, but also for all of the monastics. We aspire to share mindfulness and the teachings of liberation with everyone, and we must practice being present and available for others for long periods. While it's a joy to do this, the relentless busyness can sometimes feel overwhelming. How do we cultivate peace and share it with others?

Feeling Overwhelm in the Body

BROTHER PHAP HUU: When I'm overwhelmed, it's so easy to beat myself up and to say, "Oh my God, I've been a practitioner for so long, I should be able to handle this," or, "I'm an adult, I should have my two feet on the ground. I should be solid." When we hold positions of responsibility in the world, we may think, "I'm a leader, I'm a parent, I'm a teacher; I shouldn't feel like this." By feeling guilty about our inability to deal with a given situation, we're adding layers to an already overwhelming sensation of chaos within us.

How do we stop this cycle of blaming, judging, and criticizing ourselves? With our mindful breathing, we can learn to identify and stop our unhelpful thinking. Stopping is the first wing of meditation, and in order to really stop, we must offer ourselves a very concrete practice. We can't just say to ourselves, "Stop, don't do anything," because by saying this, we're actually pushing down and stirring up our emotions even more.

When I practice stopping, I like to come back to my body as an indicator of how I am doing. When the sensation of stress manifests, tension arises in my shoulders, in my neck, maybe in my face—perhaps my jawline is really tense, or my gaze becomes intense. Coming back to my body, I scan the different parts to see where there is tension. Sometimes the tension is in my breath. When I'm overwhelmed, my breathing can be very heavy. My chest may be tight. Listening to my body, I say to myself, "Oh, Phap Huu, your breathing's really, really tight. Why is that? What feeling are you experiencing?" And I gently allow myself to recognize the feeling; I call it by its name, I identify it.

Staying with the feeling, I start to unpack it to learn why I'm feeling overwhelmed. If we are already in touch with our feelings and our bodily sensations, this process of unpacking can happen very quickly. Sometimes it takes more time. As we start to unpack our feelings, we can ask ourselves, "Why am I overwhelmed? "What are the causes of this overwhelm?" And once I recognize the root of my emotions, I may start to feel freer already. I suddenly see what I need to address. A primary cause of my overwhelm may become clear.

This is the practice: we learn to embrace the sensation of being overwhelmed, instead of pushing it away; we may even learn to smile to ourselves and our overwhelm in recognition. We pay attention to the sensations in our body and use our breath to stay with them,

and then we start to unpack the overwhelm and identify its cause.

PRACTICE
Smiling to Our Overwhelm

BROTHER PHAP HUU: Dear friend, the first
response when we feel unable to rise to the
demands of a project or a situation is to be
mindful of that feeling; we should acknowledge
and smile to the feeling of overwhelm. Smiling to the feeling means that we're recognizing
and embracing the present reality: "I am overwhelmed." At first, smiling may feel counter-
intuitive because the feeling of overwhelm is
unpleasant—we just want it to stop. But when
we smile to our overwhelm, we create a little
space to see it differently.

We usually look for an escape when we feel
overwhelmed. We do something to try to ease our
feeling of overwhelm or to generate a more plea-
surable feeling. Running away from discomfort is
a basic habit in all of us; it's ingrained very deeply.
We want to run away from our overwhelm, from
our suffering, from the present moment.

But this is the most important moment to get in touch with our core practice of mindfulness, which means to be aware of what is happening in the here and now, whatever it is. When we start a mindfulness practice, we may develop the habit of practicing in order to feel good sensations instead of negative ones. But in the spirit of the Buddha's teachings, we practice mindfulness not to escape but to embrace everything that is happening. The way out is in.

So, when I feel overwhelmed, first of all, I stop and take a breath. I breathe in to connect my mind to my body, to focus on something other than my nonstop thinking—the countless different stories of blaming, judging, and reacting that cause me to suffer. If I leave my nonstop thinking unattended, if I don't take care of my overwhelm, it will create even more negative perceptions in my mind and tension in my body. So, the first practice, the key, is just to stop and breathe in and out with awareness.

You may like to try sitting quietly in a safe place and practice for yourself. Become aware of your breathing, and breathe with the following *gatha* or practice poem for a few moments.

Breathing in, I know I am overwhelmed.
Breathing out, I embrace the feeling of being
   overwhelmed.

With this simple practice of mindful breathing, I can recognize that I am overwhelmed and I can smile to that feeling of overwhelm. I don't see the overwhelm as something negative, but as a sign that there is something I need to address.

Embracing Our Overwhelm

JO CONFINO: It's important to be able to name the cause of our mental disturbance. My experience of overwhelm in the past is that it genuinely felt like it was filling my entire being and could quickly trigger a sense of hopelessness. This had the impact of squeezing out and neutralizing any space for a counterbalancing emotion to show up and come to my rescue.

But when I am able to name it, what I am actually doing is putting a border around the experience of overwhelm and thereby creating space around it. It's a little like a parent embracing their child when they are hurt: it immediately helps the child to feel held, and from this place of support and care, to start feeling some agency. This practice also highlights the importance of being tender with our feelings.

As Brother Phap Huu says, when we cannot cope, it is easy to feel shame or a sense of failure because we can't make things work in the way we would like. Often in this situation, we berate ourselves, sometimes even out loud. Feeling this way, we can easily touch into our childhood suffering around believing that we aren't good enough.

So, just like a mother embracing her child, we can learn to embrace our own pain and calm our fears.

Tenderness can also come from sharing our suffering with another person we trust. The saying "A problem shared is a problem halved" makes complete sense in my experience.

Through the process of writing this book, I have been experiencing my own sense of overwhelm due to a number of issues all needing my attention at the same time—including this manuscript! What has helped guide me is to watch myself during this process and notice how I have become more agitated than normal, getting stuck in a pattern where my nervous system has become more and more stimulated.

For example, normally when I eat a meal, I focus on eating, enjoying the time I have with my wife and others at the table. But during this period, there have been occasions when, in the middle of a meal, I'll get up distractedly and temporarily leave the table without speaking to Paz, my wife, because I've forgotten to make a note of what I need to do and am worried I'll forget. I've also experienced being more irritable with people, especially with my wife, because I have been feeling at the limits of my capacity—anything feels akin to the proverbial straw that breaks the camel's back. Being aware and paying attention to what is going on has definitely helped me to come back more quickly to my center.

Knowing Our Capacity and Learning When to Stop

BROTHER PHAP HUU: Often, our reaction to feeling overwhelmed is to overreact, and we thereby magnify the chaos we are already in. By trying to handle a situation that is beyond our capacity, we make matters worse because our energy is so dispersed. If our energy levels are low and our sense of overwhelm is too strong, we should recognize it's not the right time to investigate further. We may like to say to ourselves: "Oh, this is the cause of my problems, but I need space right now. I need to take care of myself. I know that it is there; it's not going anywhere. But let me take care of my well-being first." This is key. We must understand what we can handle in any given moment and we shouldn't force ourselves to proceed. If we do, we can end up feeling more powerless and we may enter a downward spiral.

This is where it becomes important to develop elements of joy and nourishment in ourselves. Even during a busy retreat—a time when we are hosting hundreds of people and there are many things to manage and attend to—I practice coming back to my body at the end of each day. I always take time to recognize and identify whether I am nourished enough to enjoy my days, and likewise to take care of difficult emotions when they arise.

I check in and ask myself: "Do I have enough nourishment—real nourishment?" Nourishment is not about skipping down the road without a care in the world; instead, it's about having enough space, time, and energy to feel stable. Sometimes, I feel balanced: I feel my mind is still, I have space, and I can embrace difficulties. When I don't feel balanced, when I recognize that I'm overwhelmed, I shouldn't engage in conversation with others—or with myself, with my own thoughts. I shouldn't give my mind the opportunity to create more stories and perceptions. Perhaps what I actually need is simply to rest, go on a walk in the forest, or drink a cup of tea alone, taking care of my stillness.

These days, many monks have Zen gardens, just as they did in generations before us. They take care of their garden—something material outside—because, in doing so, they also take care of what is inside. Gardening is a way of directing energy. The feeling of being overwhelmed is an energy, and our Zen practice is to learn to identify our energy, whatever it may be, and direct it so that it can bring us back to balance. Seen in this light, gardening with mindfulness, and even tidying up and cleaning, are not just normal actions. They're not just daily chores. They can all turn into a practice of slowing down and nourishing ourselves.

Learning to slow down and allowing ourselves to pause or to stop is so simple, but so important. In the light of Zen practice, learning to sit and be calm—not doing anything—enables us to see what is happening. This is the essence of meditation, and it's fundamental. And as Thay says, with this kind of understanding and awareness, we will know what to do and what not to do.

By stopping, we have the capacity for deep looking, or *vipassana*, insight. We have the capacity to dive into what is manifesting in the present moment. Then, because we have a practice of centering ourselves, we learn to be still, like the Zen image of a lake. When the lake is calm, it will reflect everything as it is. If a bird flies by, the bird can see itself; when the cloud passes by, the lake perfectly reflects the cloud. Our mind is the water, and most of the time it's disturbed, unable to reflect things as they are. Our mind isn't still enough to reflect reality when we are not very present.

That is why stopping comes first; it allows our mind to become still. This is the first thing we teach retreatants at Plum Village: how to stop.

A Bell of Mindfulness

BROTHER PHAP HUU: We hear many bells throughout the day in the monastery. Whether it is the great temple bell or the clock chiming in the dining hall, listening to the bell is so important—upon hearing the sound, we stop whatever we are doing and we have a moment of stillness and silence. Our inherited, ancestral habit of running is so strong in us; we feel like we always need to be doing something. Our current society reflects back that same message: we must keep going. If you're feeling upset, you may think, "Okay, because I'm agitated, I need to *do* something." Of course, this energy is not pleasant. It may be an energy of fear, anxiety, aversion, or anger, and it doesn't contribute to our deepest aspiration.

But the bell reminds us to stop and look deeply into whatever is happening within us and around us. And there is a kind of inner bell that chimes, too: we can recognize that the compulsive feeling in us to do something is itself a bell of mindfulness, offering us the insight that we are overwhelmed and agitated, reminding us to stop and breathe. When this compulsive feeling comes up, I say to myself, "Phap Huu, take a pause, come back to your breathing, feel your body, recognize the emotions and sensations that are happening in the here and now, and take care of them with tenderness. Don't push them away."

Again, it's important to notice if we have the capacity to respond to our difficult feeling in that moment. If I don't have enough strength, I say to the feeling of agitation and anxiety, "I know you're there and I'm going to take care of you, but right now I need to take care of myself." Then I may allow myself to go and rest, to practice what we call "total relaxation." When I don't have capacity for more, it's important to disconnect myself from the space or situation that is contributing to the feeling of overwhelm.

We should listen to this inner bell so that it becomes a habit in us. If you have a mindfulness practice, you can sense when your breathing becomes more agitated or harder, and there are many other ways of noticing how you are feeling. Listening like this is a good habit, one that gives us the capacity and skill to embrace all the feelings and emotions that may come up in difficult situations. And another way of saying all of this is: *Learn to listen to yourself.**

---

* You don't need to be in a monastery to be present for a bell of mindfulness. You can download a bell of mindfulness on your smartphone and program it to sound at time intervals that suit your life.

Allow Yourself Space
to Do Nothing

JO CONFINO: In my experience, by creating space and listening to ourselves, we allow inspiration to start shining through. When we busy ourselves to avoid our suffering, we close down the capacity to get in touch with the wisdom already inside of us.

I tell my coaching clients that in the work we do together, we are not going to find any of the answers to their issues outside of their own experience and inner knowing. There is a classic practice in coaching that begins by placing an empty chair next to the person receiving coaching. If they are feeling stuck or lost, you ask them to switch chairs and to get in touch with the wise elder inside of them, asking, "What would the wise part of you advise in this situation?" Each time I offer this exercise, I find that the person I am working with is able to articulate a meaningful answer that helps to change their perspective. Another tactic that helps us get out of our own way is to ask a person what their best friend would advise in any given situation. The answer is nearly always kinder, more compassionate, and more generative than the inner dialogue looping through their head.

When I worked for the *Guardian* newspaper, I used to commute to my office in London from Brighton on England's south coast. I always filled my journey with reading, working, or listening to music to avoid feeling bored. One day, I was out in the afternoon for an interview and had planned to head back to the office to pick up my bag containing my phone, computer, book, and iPod before heading home. But because of a delay, I ended up going straight to the station and left my devices at work. During the journey home, which took more than an hour, I had no choice but to just sit looking out of the window. At that time, I was feeling stuck at work and knew that I needed a new challenge. As my eyes rested on the passing woodlands and green fields, an idea popped into my head, seemingly out of nowhere, which manifested over the following months into a major project I helped spearhead.

If I had not, by chance, created that space for reflection, the idea may never have materialized. That was a real turning point in my life, and I have continued to give myself more space just to be, without the need for any particular outcome. I had previously thought that time with nothing to do equated with boredom. Since that experience, I now see "empty" time as an opportunity to get in touch with a deeper sense of knowing, to channel inspiration.

We need to get over the idea that doing nothing is a waste of time or money. We must prevent ourselves from falling into the habit of reaching for our smartphone at the merest hint of boredom in order to get a dopamine fix. I know of one friend who locks his phone in a box in the evening to physically prevent himself from checking on emails and texts. Many others, too, have learned from experience and instituted a cut-off time from their phones so as not to take their own troubles and the troubles of the world to bed with them. Try a digital detox for one evening and observe the effects on your mind, the quality of your sleep, and your life.

Develop a Practice before Life Gets Difficult

JO CONFINO: There is a story in the Old Testament about Joseph interpreting a dream of the Pharaoh to mean that seven years of plentiful crops in Egypt would lead to seven years of famine. As a result, enough grain was put aside and stored during the good times to prevent starvation when disaster struck.

In a similar fashion, it is important to develop our practice of mindfulness when times are good; if overwhelm or other troubles strike us, we will have stored up enough understanding so that we don't fall into despair. The practices in this book are a good start!

The problem is that we tend to think short-term, looking no further than the end of our nose. A lot of people say, "Oh, well, life is fine at the moment, so I don't need to invest in my spiritual practice." But actually, if we practice mindfulness when we have enough space, we can focus on better understanding how our mind really works. Then when conditions change for the worse and we lose our equanimity, we already know how to act. Without a practice, we're more likely to panic in the middle of an emergency; we can't just turn on a mindfulness switch when times are tough. The lesson is simple: develop a spiritual practice in the good times. Then, when a difficult event arises, we'll have already built good habits into our system.

Our Work Points in the Direction of Our Inner Healing

JO CONFINO: When we start paying attention to what is going on in our lives, we are able to develop the capacity to start seeing life from different perspectives. Many years ago, in a difficult moment, an insight came to me that if we look deeply into the jobs we choose and the people we work with, often they point us in the direction of the inner healing we are searching for. We project onto the world our own experiences and ways of seeing, just like an artist painting on an empty canvas, and in the same way, we also project our search for healing. For example, oftentimes someone working in a caring profession may find meaning in the work due to their own history, or they may be trying to heal the part of themselves that felt abandoned as a child.

Let me give a personal example. While at the *Guardian*, I had become concerned that as the media company grew rapidly in scale, there was an increasing risk that our core values would start to dissipate. I had already seen instances of this happening within the organization, so I made a commitment to support the *Guardian* staff in staying true to the original inspiration behind the newspaper's creation. I therefore set up a multi-year project called "Living Our Values" and set about auditing all areas of the business, spotting issues that needed addressing; for example, I noted that we were carrying sex phone line advertisements, even though this was completely counter to our position on womens' rights. At the end of the first year, I produced a public document that transparently showed how well we were performing against our values and the actions we were taking across our editorial and commercial operations to close any gaps.

Upon publication, I took the glossy pamphlet home to proudly show my then-partner, who took one look at it and said, "And when are you going to start living your own values?" At the time, after all the care and effort I had put in, her response felt like a punch to my stomach. But on reflection, I saw there was some truth in what she was saying. Spending so much time and effort to get the *Guardian* to stay true to its values, I had been projecting onto the organization my underlying concerns that I myself was not living up to my own values.

I have seen countless examples of this kind of projection. One person I coached was deeply frustrated that, despite working long hours and doing stellar work, her boss was not giving her the recognition she felt she deserved. It was only after we worked through it that she could see that she was searching for the love she had craved but not received from her parents. She had unconsciously chosen a difficult boss who couldn't offer praise, thereby perpetuating her belief that she was unlovable. When she started to transform her pain around her parents, she no longer desperately needed approval from her boss.

When we stop to think about it, we can see it is no coincidence that we end up building careers or getting into relationships hoping to heal the wounds we may carry within ourselves. But if we fail to recognize this compensatory behavior and bring it into our consciousness, then we often sustain and even deepen our patterns of suffering. Healing wounds outside of ourselves is rarely as effective as transforming them inside of ourselves. When we become mindful and gain a better understanding of the roots of our suffering, when we make peace within ourselves, we reduce our stress and are able to get grounded and start to make concrete changes all around. One of the Buddha's core teachings that has always resonated most strongly with me is that with our thoughts we create the world; changing our thoughts, the world cannot help but also change.

Can't Change the System with the Same Thinking That Created the Mess

JO CONFINO: We need to transform our worldview toward our approach to dealing with major global challenges such as climate change, biodiversity, social justice, and systems change. Like many of us, I am witnessing particularly widespread overwhelm and burnout amongst the people working in these fields. Many of them, whether they are young activists or leaders of nongovernmental organizations, feel guilty if they take any time off to relax—they feel the enormous weight of the world on their shoulders as they try to head off civilizational and ecological collapse. Many young activists, in particular, are burning out and losing faith.

This is not surprising given the scale of the challenges we are facing and the short amount of time we have to take action before it's too late. We are collectively failing to heed the warnings and radically change our behaviors toward each other and the natural world. Thay has used the metaphor of chickens in a cage fighting over the last grains, not seeing the butcher coming with his knife.

Understanding the critical importance of this moment, Plum Village has created a series of retreats for climate leaders, recognizing that at times of great stress, it is important to intentionally create space for people involved in social and environmental justice to listen deeply to each other, reflect calmly, and renew their spirit of engagement and collaboration.

Despite accepting the invitation to join these retreats, the majority of participants openly share their concern that they're being self-indulgent by taking time to look after their own well-being. Yet a central pillar of Buddhist wisdom is that we can truly be useful in the world only when we're in balance ourselves. We talk about the importance of creating a regenerative economy, but first, we need to know how to regenerate ourselves. How can we change the current extractive system with the same behaviors of striving and sacrifice that got us into this mess in the first place?

If we are constantly giving but unable to receive, then overwhelm and burnout are hard to avoid. We should be clear that it's not selfish to look after ourselves, but selfless; it's only when our own bowl is full and overflowing that we're able to give to other people. When our bowl is empty, we've got nothing to give except our sacrifice. It's the same with love: If we cannot first love ourselves, how can we truly love another person?

Walk in Freedom

JO CONFINO: Sometimes it is true that we cannot stop what we are doing, but we can always slow down, or at the very least, find moments in any day to come back to ourselves. One climate retreat participant shared how he was always rushing between meetings; for him, walking was just a means to get to the next place and was always to be done as quickly as possible. So, he looked slightly horrified when we introduced him to the core Plum Village practice of walking meditation: walking slowly, harmonizing one's steps with one's breathing, appreciating what a miracle it is to be walking on Earth, and recognizing that every step can be nourishing and healing. When he returned from his first silent walk through the Plum Village oak forest with the monastics and other retreatants, his face was lit up as though he had experienced a revelation. For the first time he could remember, he was able to allow himself to truly see the beauty around him, to listen to the birds singing and the rustling of the leaves in the wind, and to feel his feet touching the earth. He had experienced the power of the Buddhist teaching of aimlessness, which in the Plum Village practice we describe as having "nowhere to go and nothing to do." When was the last time you allowed yourself to have nothing to do, no program, no goal, no agenda? Aimlessness is one of the three doors of liberation, a gateway to awakening.*

On another occasion many years ago, I took a group of environmental leaders on a nature walk in the hills above San Francisco. I noted how they were constantly chatting. At the halfway point, I brought them together in a circle and asked them what they had noticed in the nature around them. None of them had been paying attention, and so no one had anything to offer. They got the point. On the way back we walked in silence and were able to fully enjoy the wonders around us.

In his decades-long work for peace and the environment, which took place under very difficult conditions, Thay taught the primary importance of coming home to oneself—often best done in silence. This does not have to take hours. Even if you walk in freedom for five minutes a day you can start to feel more centered and able to meet difficult situations with more grace.

---

* Thich Nhat Hanh writes on aimlessness as a gateway to freedom in *The Heart of the Buddha's Teaching: Transforming Suffering into Peace, Joy, and Liberation* (New York: Harmony, 1999), 152.

PRACTICE
Walking on the Earth

BROTHER PHAP HUU: One of the core practices in Zen is walking meditation. Sometimes when we are indoors staying in one place for a long time, we feel like we need nourishment; it could be contact with nature, or fresh air, or a change of environment, or to connect to something bigger than ourselves, such as this beautiful planet. We walk every day from one destination to the other, but we may not remember the first step we took this morning. Do we feel the contact of our feet on the earth? Walking meditation is walking with awareness of each step and each breath. Walking meditation also nourishes our joy. It teaches us how to slow down and appreciate every step.

Zen Master Thich Nhat Hanh developed what would become the Plum Village practice of walking meditation during the war in Vietnam as a response to the suffering he witnessed all around him. As a young monk, he and the other monks and nuns didn't want to contribute to the fighting and tried to find ways to bring peace instead. They formed the School of Youth for Social Service, providing aid and rebuilding bombed-out villages. As one of the few bright young monks who could speak English and French very well, Thay was sent to the United States and to other countries in the West to speak and raise awareness of what was really happening in Vietnam.

While he was in the US, he suddenly received the news that he had been exiled from Vietnam for his antiwar activities. In that moment of shock, despair, and deep suffering, he came back to his breathing. Realizing that being still in seated meditation could feel very overwhelming, he began to bring the practice of mindful breathing into walking. The mind can go in 10,000 directions from all the feelings, emotions, and difficulties that can afflict us, but as practitioners we know that we can be the master of our own mind.

Thay realized, "As long as I am alive, as long as I am still breathing, I can still arrive home anywhere on this planet. My true home is not Vietnam; my true home is in the present moment. My true home is wherever on Earth I allow myself to truly be there." This was an insight that helped him liberate himself from overwhelming feelings of isolation, disconnection, and exile. Now, he has transmitted this practice to us.

When we walk anywhere, we can practice walking meditation and bring our attention to the soles of our feet. We really feel the contact of each foot on the ground from the heel to the sole of the foot to the gentle lift of our toes pushing us a little bit forward to make the next step.

In our practice, we can combine that awareness of the movement of the soles of the feet touching the earth with the awareness of our breath. We're always breathing, so why not take advantage of our breath to be in harmony with the body? It might feel a little bit stiff at the beginning, but trust your own capacity to harmonize your breath and your steps. Trust your own ability to walk with freedom.

While you walk, let yourself really be present with each step that you take. To practice feeling at home in the present moment is a real art, but walking meditation is a practice that you can use anywhere, and you can start it right away.

Coming Home

BROTHER PHAP HUU: Rather than worrying about the future or about what's happened in the past, it is important to recognize that coming home to ourselves is the beginning of transformation. It's only when we truly stop and reflect that we can work on what's there in front of us. Of course, it is vitally important to take care of things outside of us. And because we see that the world is burning, we may think, "Who am I to have the privilege to sit calmly in meditation?" But we must realize that when we're doing any kind of climate justice work, it's equally important for us to come back to ourselves, to take care of the climate inside. Practicing like this, we create true resilience. We don't tune into our breath and our body only when we're overwhelmed—we're trying to create a practice that keeps us well for the whole journey, for our entire lives on Earth.

Coming home to ourselves is also a process of learning to be truthful and transparent with ourselves. Learning to come home is beautiful, but it can be challenging; when you come home to yourself, you start to see the ugliness inside. You see the habits that are still so alive in you that you want to transform, that you have set out on your journey to change. But they are still there. When you come home to yourself, this is an opening for what Thay calls "transformation at the base"—change at the deepest levels of the mind.

When we truly come home to ourselves, we start to reconnect to our own deep purpose, love, and compassion. And we might see that, actually, our tank of compassion is very low. We may not be able to be present for ourselves and others anymore because we have been so occupied with our external work—even if it is the good work of protecting the Earth and all that we love. We want to generate sustainability outside, but we also must generate sustainability inside.

JO CONFINO: When I ask myself, "Why did I move from New York City to rural France in order to live next door to Plum Village?" I realize it is because, for the first time in my life, I had found somewhere that I could truly call my home.

During my first-ever retreat in Plum Village back in 2010, my wife and I asked permission to be married in the main meditation hall, and Thay agreed to our request. The day after our wedding, he invited us to have tea with him. It is a moment I will never forget. When we entered his modest room, Thay was sitting on a hammock with his back to us and was being gently rocked by two attendants who were sitting on the floor. It felt like a scene that could have taken place a thousand years in the past: the Zen master and the students. Thay got up mindfully to greet us, came over, and sat next to us, making a small circle where we drank tea in silence. Then Thay turned to me and asked how I had been enjoying the past two weeks in the monastery. Without even thinking, I responded that it had been amongst the happiest times of my life. Thay asked me to explain. I said, "Thay, it is the first time in my life that I have felt able to come home to myself." I surprised myself with my own words—I had not had this thought until that moment.

After we left, I reflected on the meaning behind my words. I had two realizations. The first was that for much of my life I'd felt I was in conflict with myself. My mind was more often than not self-critical and full of worries. When something was going right, I was just waiting for it to go wrong. When I made one decision, the other part of my mind was already telling me I was making a mistake. The second insight was that because of my many insecurities, I was always on high alert out of fear of being humiliated, and I was effectively carrying a heavy suit of armor around with me. But after two weeks in Plum Village, living in mindfulness and resting within the embrace of a conscious community, I realized it was possible to live more fully at ease, to feel undefended. And to speak with my true voice. I let the suit of armor fall away. I felt lighter and more alive.

The Power of Humility

BROTHER PHAP HUU: We can't buy inner peace, balance, or wholeness. The external things that we have are conditions that can support us, but they can also become poisonous if we use them unmindfully. In our culture, we rely so much on external things to feel satisfied or at peace; exterior objects have become totally bound up with our feeling of worth, even our feeling that we exist. "Because I have this, I'm worth something, *I am someone.*" We get caught in the external aspects of our life—our possessions, yes, but also our work, our status in society, who we imagine ourselves to be—and we lose touch with the real sources of our energy. If we continue to behave in this disconnected way, we will lose ourselves completely, and we will burn out. We have witnessed this in our friends, our colleagues, and we've even seen it in our own Plum Village community.

JO CONFINO: I'd like to offer a couple of anecdotes about the dangers of looking for external recognition and puffing ourselves up. We want to create a good impression on others, but sometimes our behavior is based on an intrinsic sense of not being good enough and we look outward for validation and proof that we're worthy of love. Once I was asked to facilitate a two-day sustainability conference in Amsterdam with 1,300 participants. I arrived with a colleague and as we walked through the main entrance of the conference center, I was stopped twice in quick succession, once because someone asked for a photo with me and the other time by a delegate wanting my autograph. My colleague turned to me as we walked on and said, incredulously: "Wow, Jo, you're famous." It's hard to describe exactly the impact of his words, but suddenly I felt that I had expanded beyond my sense of self—that I was more than who I was—and it felt *great*. I was now famous; I had made it. It was almost as though all my insecurities suddenly evaporated and I had grown into being a new, more powerful, and more confident person.

All this happened in an instant. Luckily, I had the wherewithal to recognize that I wasn't experiencing a wonder drug, but a poison, one that would lead only to disaster if I were to fall into the trap of believing it. I was a balloon being pumped full of air: at some point, the pressure would become too great and I would suddenly pop with a loud bang, ending up feeling even more insecure than before.

We see this phenomenon happening over and over again in the world with so-called celebrities suffering from various addictions, sometimes even driven to suicide as they attempt to cope with the intoxicating power that comes with fame. To expunge this poison from my system, I shared the story with a number of people over the coming days. By voicing it and being transparent about it, I wanted to really understand the experience and let go of this idea that fame would improve my life and make me happy.

On another occasion, I attended a large environmental gathering in Sydney, Australia, the World Parks Congress of the International Union for Conservation of Nature (IUCN). I arrived to find that, unusually for a journalist, I had been given VIP status. This meant carrying around my neck the oversized official convention tag emblazoned with a large red VIP symbol, while nearly all of the other 5,000 participants wore a simple "delegate" sign. I have to admit that at first, it felt good to be marked out as being different from the crowd; delegates responded to me in a more deferential manner than usual and I could retreat at any time to the VIP lounge, where I could eat fine cakes and mix with other very important people. But then I discovered that there was an even smaller group of people with black VIP tags, which meant they were even more important than I was. How I hankered after one of those! Fortunately, just like the time in Amsterdam, I was able to see through this ego-driven haze and recognize the falsehood of these feelings. Wearing the VIP badge paradoxically meant I felt needy to be noticed and therefore separate from those around me.

By searching for power outside of ourselves, not only do we hide and therefore exacerbate our inner insecurities; we also give rise to a sense of entitlement. With this entitlement, we believe we deserve the benefits that accrue from our place in society, rather than seeing our social position as a way to be in service to others. Our greatest protection from our ego taking control is to maintain our humility.

Taking Care of the Fire Within

BROTHER PHAP HUU: Rather than looking outside ourselves for validation, we know a deeper feeling of connection comes from living more simply and as mindfully as we can. In Plum Village, we eat, walk, talk, and even sleep with a sense of awareness of what we are doing. Cultivating mindfulness in this way, it's important to remember that I can close the door more gently, I can walk more slowly, and I can speak more softly, but if I'm not taking care of the anger and frustration inside by easing up, recognizing the different energies in me, and taking care of them, then at some point I'm going to break; all of these emotions will just take me over.

All of our inner transformation is manifested in our bodily actions, in how we interact with the world outside. If you have a deep aspiration to save the planet or make the world a better place, but you are burning inside with the fire of frustration, anger, resentment or hatred, then those energies will express themselves in your speech and your bodily actions in ways you can't control—even without your knowing it. Your anger will ruin the possibility of good communication; harmony and goodwill within your team will erode; your most precious relationships will break. Harboring these energies, we are not who we want to be and we aren't in control.

Toward the end of a retreat in Canada for climate leaders, one of the participants—someone who had been fighting against the destructive tar sands industry for nearly two decades—shared a deep insight related to this point. He said, "I have been angry for so long about the destruction wrought by the extraction of oil from the tar sands that I have become an angry and bitter man." Because he had not taken care of the energy of anger, it had become a habit, a default response that carried across all aspects of his life. Our habit energies are like a horse galloping at full speed, carrying us away without us knowing where we're going. Fortunately, with mindfulness, we gain the chance to have a life-changing insight about our habitual behaviors and can choose a different path.

After each retreat we hold, nearly all participants express that they will take the practice of deep listening with them and apply it in their daily lives. And they know that they must first listen deeply to themselves, to embrace all their feelings and emotions, and to recognize when they need support—we always recommend that people find a sangha, a circle of friends with whom to practice.

Like them, we should pause, look at our deepest aspirations, and ask ourselves, "Do I still have the energy to continue? Do I need support, or do I have the right support? Do I need to find a friend who can support me?"

Simple Commitments
Can Change the World

JO CONFINO: Let's build on what Brother Phap Huu mentioned earlier about living a simpler life. We are so stuck in our habit of striving that we often adopt the same mindset when we're looking for a way out of our difficulties. We tend to think that because we deal with so much complexity in our day-to-day lives, the way to greater peace must also require a sophisticated and complex response. But the paradox is that the most effective response to complexity is often simplicity.

At the end of retreats, the monastics sometimes ask participants to make a commitment to change something in their lives—an achievable, sometimes humble change that they feel confident experimenting with. For example, one young woman who enjoyed the practice of mindful eating committed not to watch Netflix while preparing and eating her meals. Feeling the peace of walking in mindfulness, another retreatant vowed to take breaks throughout the day and go for short walks. One person committed to walking in freedom from his kitchen to his home office once a week—a journey of less than thirty meters. On the surface, this last commitment could appear to be the tiniest of steps, both literally and metaphorically, with little chance of creating a positive impact. But the greater truth is that by walking even a short distance in this way, he would gain a real taste of what it is to be free. The insight that comes when we touch freedom cannot be restricted to that one small action alone but gently ripples out into our entire understanding of life.

It is important we don't bring our busyness into the realm of our spiritual practice. At the end of one retreat, a climate scientist approached me and reeled off a long list of the changes he planned to make in his life—all at the same time—and asked me for feedback. I responded that he was at risk of overwhelming himself and ending up feeling he had failed. Instead, it would be best to start with one small step and to recognize that within one practice are all practices. He quickly reduced his list to something more manageable and more likely to be sustainable over time.

During retreats, the monastics offer a period of "total relaxation" after lunch. Retreatants come to the main meditation hall and lie down on cushions while one of the monks or nuns leads a guided meditation, including a body scanning exercise: participants are asked to pay attention to each part of the body in turn, noticing and releasing any stress along the way, and just rest. This practice is often very impactful for the retreatants. Taking forty-five minutes to stop, come back to their body, and let everything else go feels like a revolutionary act when the whole of our culture and society is based on always running and doing.

When I ask retreatants "What brings you joy?" or "What keeps you feeling peaceful and grounded?" an overwhelming majority don't respond with answers such as "going on vacation," "having a fancy dinner," or "buying a new car." The most popular responses refer to the simple pleasures of life: "I like to connect with nature." "I like to go for a walk." "I like to just sit somewhere quietly." All of these responses speak about being calm, being quiet, being present, and doing just one thing rather than trying to multitask. Truthfully, even in the midst of busyness, we can choose one small thing to help us return to a greater sense of balance.

With coaching clients, I will sometimes suggest that they get a cookie jar and write on a number of strips of paper: "I give myself permission to …" Every time they choose to do something for their well-being, they fill in the gap on the paper, such as "I give myself permission to take a ten-minute walk outside" or "I give myself permission to stop work at 5:00 p.m. today" and pop it in the jar. Over time the jar starts to fill up and this slow accumulation of "self-love notes" helps give them confidence that it is possible to prioritize their own needs while also getting stuff done.

It's also important to recognize that practices such as deep listening, compassionate speech, mindful eating, walking meditation, and total relaxation do not take years of practice to put into action. You can start straight away and they will immediately have an impact. And the more we practice them, the deeper the impact will be.

Eco-Anxiety and
Taking Refuge in the Earth

JO CONFINO: Sometimes our feelings of overwhelm come not from the many things we are trying to achieve in the present moment, but from our fears about the future. As we face the cataclysmic impacts of the climate emergency, this is especially true for young people, some of whom are even deciding not to have children because they do not believe that a positive future is possible for humanity.

In the nearly thirty years I worked for the *Guardian* and the HuffPost, my focus was on climate and sustainability, and I was constantly reminded of the epic nature of the challenges we face and the ongoing lack of an appropriate collective response. The rapid rise in extreme weather events, the extinction of many thousands of species, and growing levels of human suffering all contributed to a great deal of grief in me and occasional despair. The insights I gained from my many interviews with Thay over the years for the *Guardian* were instrumental in helping me to develop the strength of mind to be able to both look this suffering in the eye and hold on to a sense of hope. I learned that truly letting go of the need to save the planet from the worst impacts of climate change can paradoxically help us to achieve that very aim.

Thay was able to talk about the collapse of this civilization with an air of calm and acceptance, grounded in mindfulness and insight. He said to me:

> Without collective awakening, the catastrophe will come. Civilizations have been destroyed many times and this civilization is no different. It can be destroyed. We can think of time in terms of millions of years and life will resume, little by little. The cosmos operates for us very urgently, but geological time is different. If you meditate on that, you will not go crazy. You accept that this civilization could be destroyed and life will begin later on after a few thousand years because this is something that has happened in the history of this planet.
>
> When you have peace in yourself and accept that the worst could happen, then you are calm enough to do something, but if you are carried by despair, there is no hope. It's like the person who is struck with a terminal illness and they learn they have been given one year or six months to live. They suffer very much and fight. But if they come to accept that they will die and they prepare to live every day peacefully and they

enjoy every moment, the situation may change
and the illness may go away. That has happened
to many people.

Thay talked about how people spend much of their lives
worrying and feeling overwhelmed about getting ill,
aging, and losing the things they treasure most, despite the
obvious fact that one day they will have to let them all go.

"When we understand that we are more than our
physical bodies, that we didn't come from nothingness
and will not disappear into nothingness, we are liberated
from fear," he told me. "Take refuge in Mother Earth
and surrender to her and ask her to heal us, to help us.
We have to accept that the worst may happen, that most
of us will die as a species and many other species will die
also, and Mother Earth will still be capable to bring us
out again."

PRACTICE
The Five Remembrances

When we find peace in ourselves and accept
the nature of impermanence, we can still cultivate gratitude and appreciation even as we know
we may be dying. One of the daily practices in

Plum Village is to recite and meditate on the Five Remembrances to cultivate the understanding and acceptance of impermanence.

> I am of the nature to grow old. There is no way to escape growing old.
>
> I am of the nature to have ill-health. There is no way to escape having ill-health.
>
> I am of the nature to die. There is no way to escape death.
>
> All that is dear to me and everyone I love are of the nature to change. There is no way to escape being separated from them.
>
> I inherit the results of my actions of body, speech, and mind. My actions are my continuation.

Meditating on the Five Remembrances regularly can help us place all our feelings of busyness, overwhelm, and burnout in perspective; it can help us find a way out of despair to Right Action, the practice of nonviolence toward ourselves and others. Together with practicing self-love and our simple commitments to change, we can touch a sense of freedom as we go about our daily lives.

The Spaciousness of Silence

BROTHER PHAP HUU: Noble silence is another powerful and truly nourishing practice. Interestingly, it's also the practice that many people feel most nervous about at the beginning of a retreat. Noble silence begins in our retreats at 9:30 p.m., and it carries on until after breakfast the next morning. In some retreats it can last until lunchtime. That's a long time for most people to experience and practice silence!

The dominant culture in our society equates silence with boredom. Silence is awkward, we think, so our environment should always be noisy. There should always be music playing in the background, even at restaurants; we turn the TV on so that there is some white noise at all times. We have created a culture that is always "switched on."

However, our friends share that, after they get over the initial shock when they first arrive, the silence is *delicious*. The silence allows us to be with ourselves. One friend shared that he even started to get nervous as the silence was about to end each morning; he suddenly realized, "Oh my gosh, I have to talk to someone now!" Actually, after the period of noble silence ends, you don't *have* to talk to anyone. If you want to continue the silence, it is there. That silence is always present. But outside the monastery, as a culture we have collectively created a lifestyle in which the norm is to chat all the time—we have become afraid of silence, and we need to transform our relationship to it. Noble silence is one of the most precious gifts we can offer ourselves.

We practice formal meditation early in the morning because there's something very sacred about this time; it's when the day is just beginning, and our energy is very fresh. Speaking for myself, I am most awake at that early morning time. My energy is starting up, and my mind is very calm. Many other monasteries also practice formal meditation in the morning with the energy of the sunrise. It's like we're waking up with the Earth; we are the Earth waking up. Even during our "lazy" days—our rest days when we don't have to get up for the morning meditation—I still enjoy the silence. After twenty years of monastic life, I don't really need an alarm clock. I wake up automatically around 5:00 a.m., sometimes even earlier, and I allow myself to enjoy the morning by becoming one with the silence.

This habit of silence has had a very deep effect on me. The capacity to be at ease with silence is a type of freedom—a way to be with ourselves and to find inner peace. Our true nature, our aspirations, our fears, our habits, our despair, all begin to express themselves in the silence. In the silence, all our mental formations have the space to arise; with our practice, we can be present with and take care of them.

JO CONFINO: The first time I discovered what you call the deliciousness of silence, I was in my thirties. I attended a ten-day silent Vipassana retreat in the UK. At the time, everyone thought that I would hate it because I am such a social person and *love* to be in conversation. So, it came as a surprise even to me that underneath my need for attention was another part of me that just wanted to *be*. Actually, it came as a huge relief not to have to think about engaging in conversation, not to worry if I sounded intelligent enough, or not to be compulsively alert to any awkward silences, quickly thinking of what the next topic of conversation should be. It was the first time I had experienced what you describe as the ability to pay attention to the small things in life, which I normally would not have noticed, and to realize they have great value.

That ability to refocus my attention in this way has been so helpful in my life. When I moved to New York City to work at the HuffPost, my walk into work was filled with the noise of construction and the honking of car horns. I felt quite overwhelmed by the constant din. One day I was on my way to the office and beyond the din, I heard a bird singing in one of the few trees along the sidewalk. By retuning my hearing to be present for the bird, its song became louder and the din started to fade away a little. From that day on, I was often able to quieten the noise of human doings and tune into the being of the birds. My walk to work became a meditative practice.

The Power of Presence

BROTHER PHAP HUU: Thay taught that in order to have a balanced monastic life, every day should include practice, study, service, and joy. Our monastic training is based on these four elements.

1. First, the practice—Dharma practice—means to practice mindfulness, concentration, and insight and to apply the teachings on love and compassion to situations in our daily lives.

2. Study, the second element, is not just textbook study. We must study life: we study our experience and we learn from our interactions with other people and with nature.

3. The third element is service, by which we mean that we want to contribute to something positive, whether that is our own inner growth or tending to our community, our loved ones, or to society. A "contribution" doesn't need to be something grand; actually, we're always contributing with our presence. A smile is a

contribution. Someone who knows how to be with themselves, who is peaceful, solid, and free, is contributing these qualities to the world.

4. The fourth and last element is joy, or play. If we don't taste the joy of meditation, then we are practicing in the wrong way. Joy has many layers. Sometimes I just sit outside on the deck of Thay's Sitting Still Hut, where he used to live, and I look out over the forest, recognizing the simple perfection of life. I feel so joyful and so grateful to be alive. We all have sources of joy in our life. But are we mindful enough to be present for them, to receive them?

These are four nourishing elements that are always there for us. We can only enjoy these elements—practice, study, service, and joy—with true presence. That is why, in our practice of mindfulness, we must also learn to be present. Many of us are absent from our own lives, unable to appreciate the many conditions for happiness we may already have. But when we are mindful, there is a power of presence. This presence—the capacity to show up and be there—is critical now more than ever.

JO CONFINO: Many people mistake presence with doing nothing, because they have become caught in the trap of believing that "doing" is what's most important in our lives and that "being" is a distant second.

Not long ago, while facilitating a training workshop for the senior executives of a large Nordic company, one of the directors shared a deep insight: "I realize that from the moment I wake up to the moment I go to sleep, I fill every single second of that time with doing something," he said. The workshop was the culmination of a journey to help the team become more emotionally intelligent, find ways to listen to each other, and collaborate more effectively. This particular executive, after recognizing on the last afternoon that he was actually fearful of creating space in his life, made the following commitment: "I'm going to spend fifteen minutes every evening just staring at a wall."

This may not be the most effective way of doing nothing, but it was extraordinary nonetheless to see him wrestle with his established pattern of living. Before that workshop, I'd never met someone who wouldn't allow themselves even a moment of quiet and rest in their lives. Living like that, you can't help yourself without some outside intervention. You can't possibly get in touch with yourself. You're constantly running away.

Get Real:
Bringing Presence to Difficult Conversations

BROTHER PHAP HUU: Presence is vital for getting in touch with ourselves, but it's also particularly important for reconciliation when difficulties arise in relationships. Perhaps you may be surprised to hear that disagreements occur even within the monastery—sometimes opinions differ, or a particular issue might touch our suffering. Instead of fretting that our suffering is coming to the surface, we should resolve things in a way that everyone feels they have been heard and respected.

Here's an example: after some rifts occurred between us monastics during a recent retreat, we held a five-hour team building session to reconcile. Some of us had disappointments, regrets, and even feelings of overwhelm about how things had happened or not happened during the retreat. But because we were able to be so present, we could be real with one another; we could express how we truly felt and at the same time not stick with a view just because we wanted to be right.

As everyone who works in a team knows, sharing honest feedback mindfully and kindly is essential to transform difficulties. But at the same time, speaking up can be difficult; we are sometimes afraid of being unable to express ourselves skillfully, afraid of hurting others' feelings or being overwhelmed by our own emotions. We may also be scared of another person's imagined anger or disappointment. Understanding may be the basis of love, but skillful communication is also critical; without it, we can't begin to move through conflicts. For this reason, deep listening and loving speech are as integral a part of our mindfulness practice as sitting meditation.

Nonetheless, as we know, spiritually bypassing difficult emotions can seem so much easier than transforming them together. If we hadn't been truly present with one another at the team building session, I don't think we could have untangled all of the knots that had accumulated between us. In general, when team members don't bring their authentic presence, the group might say, "All right, that wasn't the best experience it could have been, but *whatever*. Let's just move on." In those cases, we don't want to be present, we don't want to be with one another, and we stop being real. Over time, this kind of bypassing erodes a group's sense of unity and leads to gradual separation.

Learning to be present with others is also learning to take care of our own feelings of overwhelm. To transform this energy of overwhelm requires us to turn it back inwards, to truly see it and work with it. Because all of us in that session had been practicing mindfulness, deep listening, and loving speech for a long time, we each had developed our presence sufficiently to work through our difficulties.

That is not to say that strong feelings didn't come up. In fact, things got quite heated at the three-hour mark, but we had the presence of mind to respond appropriately. We gave ourselves a fifteen-minute break to each do our own walking meditation outside. It was a beautiful moment—we knew taking a pause wasn't an act of running away from an uncomfortable conversation, but an act of deep caring for ourselves and one another. We recognized that we didn't have the capacity to listen anymore.

During the time I was walking, I felt great love for the whole group and a clear sense of mutual respect. After our walk, we continued to speak and listen for another two hours, reaching a deep sense of understanding and reconciliation. It was a mind-blowing experience: the sense of connection between us all was palpable in the tears, the hugs, and the smiles that manifested later.

Collective Transformation

BROTHER PHAP HUU: Sharing our feelings can be an overwhelming experience; when we are flooded with strong emotions, it can be scary to feel them, let alone express them. Within families, at the workplace, or in school, there will always come a moment when we come up against our emotional limit.

In this particular meeting for our retreat organizing team, we recognized our collective sense of overwhelm and said, "We have to come together, to be there for each other and listen to each other." We made a commitment to move through our difficulties together.

1. The first step we took was to recognize the need to transform our suffering *together*.

2. Secondly, it was important not to rush the process and to give everyone a chance to express themselves and feel heard. Some people have the confidence to speak right away, while others need time and encouragement to say what is in their hearts. We recognized that we would come

together and listen to one another no matter how long it took.

3. And when we felt that it was all too much, we took a break so that each of us individually could come back to the practice of mindfulness and regain our presence. In this particular example, we all went for a walk.

4. After the walk, we returned to the process with our trust intact—we gave each other a nod and we continued.

I believe that if we hadn't come together in that way, that knot would have remained present in each of us; it would have carried through to the next big retreat and into that summer teaching season. By stopping and dealing with it straight away, we did not give our feelings the chance to fester and infect the whole community.

The opportunity to practice mindfulness is always there. Mindfulness doesn't belong only in the meditation hall or in the monastery. It can be in any space. It is there in silence and in speaking.

Vulnerability Is the
Opening to Possibility

JO CONFINO: Taking a break from an intense conversation but keeping the intention to continue is very powerful. Stopping means "I'm no longer prepared to keep pushing in a direction I know is going to create more harm," while at the same time acknowledging to oneself that "I'm no longer going to run away." This is the gateway into showing up with vulnerability. Being vulnerable is a crucial aspect of dealing with overwhelm: we often feel the need to close down and protect ourselves to cope with a difficult situation, but actually healing often comes from opening up and allowing something new to emerge.

When we share authentically from the heart, we become more present. By having the courage to take off our armor and show our scars, we give other people permission to do the same. A space and connection between us that wasn't there before has an opportunity to come into being. I use the metaphor of a tuning fork: when one tuning fork vibrates, it causes an identical one to also start "singing."

We should of course be careful that we're in a safe, trusted space when we are being vulnerable. Having facilitated and been part of many group sharings over the years, I have seen time and again that when one person is able to share their deep feelings, others also feel safer to share.

We are more able to be open and vulnerable when we come out of our comfort zone and stop hiding behind our defense mechanisms or our armor, whether that's our status, expertise, or age. The first Plum Village Climate Leaders' Retreat in 2023 brought together people with starkly different views on how to address the climate emergency. Some retreatants fundamentally agreed with one solution, while others opposed it and strongly believed in a different approach. How did the monastics create the conditions for these experts and leaders to slow down and actually listen to each other, rather than triggering their usual behavior of immediately jumping to judgments?

Here's what they *didn't* do. When I've attended mainstream climate conferences in the past, I've received the full schedule in advance, plus the bios of everyone attending. For the more sophisticated conferences, I would receive pre-networking opportunities in the conference app, so that I could skim through the list and get in touch with people ahead of time to plan appointments. This meant that before I even set foot in the conference itself, I was already making judgments that would influence my experience. *What sessions do I want to go to? Whom do I want to speak to? Who might help me with my project? Whom do I want to avoid? Which of my friends will be present? Who's there whom I can approach for funding?* etc., etc.

But in Plum Village, it was the opposite. The retreat facilitators didn't send out the schedule or attendee information in advance. When people turned up, the monastics had the participants use only their first names, without putting the organization they were associated with on their nametags. In effect, they were asking people to let go of their identities and trust the process. This way of organizing meant that the climate leaders turned up with a sense of curiosity and openness; they came as themselves, as human beings rather than "human doings" primarily identified with their roles.

One of the most powerful aspects of the retreat was that for the first three days there was no discussion on the actual topic at hand. The daily schedule—meditation, walking in nature, and communal eating in silence—encouraged people just to get to know each other as human beings, to appreciate and listen to each other. These first three days provided retreatants the opportunity to be vulnerable, and this vulnerability created a sense of community—a sense that we are all in this together and that the most important thing, below surface disagreements, is to support each other.

There was even a moment when one participant, a leader in the movement to close down the fossil fuel industry, rested her head unknowingly on the shoulder of a senior executive of an oil and gas company. As she recounted later, this just would not have happened if she had known in advance what he did for a living; she would have avoided him and thus also missed the opportunity to have a transformational conversation.

These connections meant that during the substantive, issue-based discussions during the final two days of the retreat, retreatants could relax and be present for each other. One climate leader spoke about how liberating this was: what she found so difficult in traditional business settings was that as soon as she opened her mouth, she felt people were already judging her. But she recognized also in that moment that her habit was to do the very same thing—she instantly formed a view about what was right and wrong.

Often when we feel overwhelmed, we feel alone, unsafe, and like the world is our enemy. We want to hide away. But a secret of dealing with busyness and overwhelm is to allow these difficult feelings to come out of hiding. If we shy away from painful feelings, we only exacerbate our sense of isolation, which in turn intensifies our overwhelm. We're not letting anyone offer their support and care to us because we've closed the door.

BROTHER PHAP HUU: Learning to be vulnerable is the key. I have now unlocked that capacity in myself to be open, to accept help, to be vulnerable. I have learned to express myself, to cry, and to accept the tears, especially after Thay's passing. That post-retreat monastic meeting is a perfect example of how vulnerability allows us to truly connect with one another. Those conversations were transformative for me. Vulnerability is not a weakness; it's a real strength. It's a real way in.

JO CONFINO: Being vulnerable in a safe space, we allow ourselves to crack open. When we show ourselves more fully and let others see the cracks in our armor, we realize, as Leonard Cohen famously sang, "that's how the light gets in." Rather than the world ending, we touch our tender heart. I liken it to being in a dark room and seeing the shadow of a giant scary monster on the wall cast by the light of a lamp. We want to run away because we feel like we're in danger. But turning toward the light and moving closer to it, we see that the monster is just the shadow of a friendly mouse. In the same way—by turning toward and moving closer—we can befriend our fears.

Many of the world's problems are caused by each of us striving to be the perfect individual, hiding our weaknesses, and presenting ourselves as strong and able to take what we want out of life. This kind of striving is a key driver in the crisis of individuation and overcon-sumption we're in. We're damaging the world because we're causing damage to ourselves. What we're creating outside is a reflection of what we're creating inside.

The Island of the Self

BROTHER PHAP HUU: The Buddha taught many times that we each have an island inside of us, a space to come back to and take refuge in. Some of us, when we start our spiritual journey, need a teacher to show us the way, to guide us with practices that we can develop. But it is also important to develop the teacher inside so that we can always take refuge within ourselves.

Here's a story about that: When Sariputra and Maha Maudgalyayana, two of the Buddha's greatest disciples, had just passed away, he called all of his monks and nuns together, looked at them, and said, "With the passing of Sariputra and Maha Maudgalyayana, it feels like there is a big gap in the community. The feeling of emptiness is there because these two monastics were such a solid presence. But you know, even I—your teacher, the Buddha—will have to go one day. Isn't that just how life is? In a mighty tree, the larger branches that support us will one day rot and collapse. This is only natural. But the younger sprouts will still be there. And that is why all of you—monastic practitioners and laypeople—must learn to take refuge in yourself, in your island of Dharma, your island of practice."

This story highlights how the Buddha taught us to take refuge in ourselves. It also demonstrates the Buddha's ability to be vulnerable. Even the Buddha, an enlightened and awakened being whom everybody respected, felt an emptiness when two of his senior students passed away. He took time to address his community because he knew that there was grief among the community members.

More than 2,500 years later, we can ask ourselves a concrete question: What is our island of practice? In Plum Village, it is the practice of mindful breathing; our walking meditation; our practice of coming home to smile to, embrace, and take care of whatever arises in the present moment. It is so important to find and to develop that island of practice within ourselves. To highlight this for our first group of climate retreatants, we asked everyone at the retreat's opening to share one practice that helps to ground them. It may sound cliché, but three quarters of the monastics in attendance shared that their mindful breathing is the one reliable place of refuge that nobody can take away.

This is true for me too: because it is so integral to our tradition, the practice of the Sixteen Exercises of

Mindful Breathing has become my island, my deepest refuge.* In any situation—whatever is happening, whoever I am meeting—I practice awareness of my breathing. When I'm listening to something being shared that is painful for me or for my brothers or sisters, I've learned to recognize and take care of my emotions by coming back to my mindful breathing. This recognition feels like a loved one's palm gently stroking the back of the young, reactive child within me and soothing him. We can take refuge like this in our island right away.

The island within us can always grow. This growth is organic, but it depends on our efforts. Our island flourishes only if we invest time and energy into spiritual practices like mindful breathing, sitting in stillness, mindful walking, total relaxation, having a cup of tea, enjoying the sunrise, enjoying the sunset. It's not selfish to enjoy quality moments like these—others will benefit from your freshness. Once you have tasted such stillness and inner peace, you have faith in yourself, in your island—and you'll know that you can touch these elements within you at any moment.

---

* Within the Sixteen Exercises of Mindful Breathing are four groupings: the first set has the body as the object of full awareness; the second has the feelings; the third, the mind; and the fourth, the objects of the mind. To read more, see *Breathe! You Are Alive* (Parallax Press, 2008) for Thich Nhat Hanh's commentary on these exercises.

Pain and Poetry:
A Zen Master's Example

BROTHER PHAP HUU: One of the reasons I consider Thay to be a great teacher is that he reached a state of great peace and presence in his life despite facing so many obstacles, including campaigning for peace during the war in Vietnam and then his exile from his homeland for thirty-nine years. Even after the foundation of Plum Village in 1982, there were challenging conditions. In 2009, his newly ordained monastics in Vietnam were forced to flee the country for their own safety.

I saw Thay face many situations that could easily have led others into despair. I can tell you in two words how Thay remained calm under acutely painful circumstances: walking meditation. When the monasteries in Vietnam were going through difficult times, Thay resourced himself by going outside in nature; as Thay's attendant, I went with him. On those walks, I was aware that Thay likely suffered just as much as—maybe more than—my brothers and sisters in Vietnam. As a teacher, he felt responsible for his students' safety and welfare. Walking meditation became his island, a way to come back to himself and take care of the feelings and emotions that were arising. We didn't talk as we walked, but I could sense through nonverbal communication, through his presence, that he was paying attention to all that was coming up in him and around him.

There is a path in Plum Village that leads from the main monks' residence at Upper Hamlet to the much smaller Son Ha Monastery, which Thay named "the legendary footpath." It's a very beautiful walk through the pine trees. Once, while walking behind Thay on this path, I knew—without Thay telling me—that his footsteps were those of his teacher. As he walked, he placed his feet lightly yet very intentionally on the earth. Walking in his teacher's footsteps was a practice for Thay; each step was a place of grounding and refuge for him. When we channel our energy like Thay did during that walk, clarity manifests right away.

During this period of disturbance in Vietnam in 2009, using the suffering in himself and around him as a focus for his practice, Thay wrote amazing letters to us, his students, to help us process our own suffering. He shared that the situation was a wake up bell for Vietnam and a chance for all of us to see how much suffering still existed in the world. Writing these letters, Thay was very aware that a kind and encouraging word would go a long way toward helping his students.

Thay wrote by hand to us twice a year—each monastic received a copy, a very personal gift from teacher to student. Since the summer family retreat is our busiest season in Plum Village, we always received a letter from Thay during that period. At that retreat, we offer 120 percent of ourselves: cooking, giving Dharma talks, presentations, 1:1 consultations, and generally working nonstop. As our teacher, Thay was deeply aware that his students were going above and beyond, giving so much of themselves to everyone; he knew that we needed a shot of vitamin C—C for compassion! In his letters during this busy time, Thay sometimes reminded us that with presence, mindfulness, and compassion, we can offer the other person our smile, and a smile can bloom on their face right away. It doesn't take years of effort to have an impact on the world; through your presence, your impact is right here, right now.

In the 1970s, Thay was holding a lot of suffering; during this time he wrote some of his most profound poetry. For me, one line from the poem "Recommendation" will always stand out: "Man is not our enemy." This line is my North Star. It helps me not to lose my equanimity when I'm experiencing anger. When we see that it is ignorance that guides another person's actions, the desire to punish or destroy them falls away; instead, we want to help them get free of that ignorance. Here is the full poem:

Recommendation

Promise me,
promise me this day,
promise me now,
while the sun is overhead
exactly at the zenith,
promise me:
Even as they
strike you down
with a mountain of hatred and violence;
even as they step on you and crush you
like a worm,
even as they dismember and disembowel you,
remember brother, remember:
man is not our enemy.
The only thing worthy of you is compassion –
invincible, limitless, unconditional.
Hatred will never let you face
the beast in man.
One day, when you face this beast alone
with your courage intact, your eyes kind,
untroubled
(even as no one sees them),
out of your smile

will bloom a flower.
And those who love you
will behold you
across ten thousand worlds of birth and dying.
Alone again,
I will go on with bent head,
knowing that love has become eternal.
On the long, rough road
the sun and moon will continue to shine.

We have to be the compassion, the understanding, that we want to see in the world. Even if the other side doesn't have understanding, we shouldn't become another victim of their suffering; they are already the first victim of their own suffering and wrong view. With the practice of mindfulness, Thay generated the clarity needed to look at a situation in a new light.

In addition to walking and writing, Thay was often nourished by his practice of calligraphy. He really enjoyed the whole process: making a cup of tea, drinking it in mindfulness, and then pouring a little bit of the tea in the ink. Then he would cut the rice paper, set up the table, and one at a time, write a phrase meant to inspire deep practice: words to meditate on like "Are you sure?" or "The tears I shed yesterday have become rain."

In Zen, there are traditions of calligraphy, flower-arranging, playing an instrument, or even just tidying up and sweeping the floor. Each of these activities can be an art, a path of discovery, and a journey to the truth. This is something we can all do. You can generate activities like this to nourish yourself. Activities to cultivate our Zen mind are things that relax us and promote focus, not things that help us run away from suffering. I don't mean a computer screen to forget yourself in, or an absorbing Netflix series, or losing yourself listening to music. Instead, I mean activities that bring us back to the present moment, activities that encourage clarity and insight.

The New Way Is the Ancient Way: Ripening, Reciprocity, and Regeneration

JO CONFINO: While modern culture prizes speed, efficiency, individuation, and extraction, ancient wisdom values patience, flow, and reciprocity, recognizing that if we tend to other people and the land, they will tend to us in turn. This circular flow of energy is regenerative in nature; we show our generosity to life and life expresses its generosity to us.

This means that when we take action, it is from a place where we feel fresh and inspired. We can have clarity and determination and at the same time experience joy, patience, and trust. *Those* are the gifts that we need to bring to the world, not more busyness, more overwhelm, more guilt, or other kinds of mental anguish—the world already has enough of those.

The importance of patience is reflected within the four Dharma Seals that Thay created as a way of knowing the hallmarks of an authentic Plum Village teaching. The fourth one, called "Ripening moment by moment," has a particular resonance when we want to minimize the risk of falling into the pit of overwhelm and burnout.[*]

Ripening is the understanding that change does not happen immediately; the care, love, attention, and commitment we put into what's important in life takes time to mature. Life is not like instant noodles. Our ability to transform suffering is the journey of a lifetime; more precisely, it's a journey of *lifetimes*—we hand the baton over to the next generation, just as the previous generations have handed it to us. But modern culture is based on the expectation that we take a particular action to see a particular result, and preferably as quickly as possible. This is exacerbated by the contraction in many peoples' attention span—content creators now work with the premise that videos should be limited to thirty seconds so no one watching becomes bored.

This fast-paced, results-driven perspective denies the truth that life is complex. It may be that an action we take now does not mature for years or even in our lifetime. One of my brothers told me the story of meeting a seventy-year-old farmer who was planting oak saplings in Portugal. He asked the man why he was planting trees

---

[*] The Four Dharma Seals of Plum Village are: "I have arrived, I am home," "Go as a river," "The times (past, present, and future) and the truths (the Four Noble Truths and also the conventional and ultimate truths) inter-are," and "Ripening, moment-by-moment."

that he would not see mature in his lifetime, and the man answered that this was precisely the reason—he was planting trees for future generations.

Every thought we have, every word we utter, every action we take flows out into the world and into eternity and we cannot know its impact. When you throw a pebble into a pond, you see the ripples go out in every direction. Even when you can't really see them, they're still there, stretching out further and further.

A story my mother told me illustrates this process. A long time ago, my mother used to take our neighbor's young daughter, Julie, on trips to London because the girl's parents had been too busy for family trips to the city. On a few occasions, my mother had taken Julie to the Victoria and Albert museum (V&A), whose collection spans 5,000 years of art. Around twenty years later, there was a knock on my parents' door; Julie had come to pay my mother a visit and offer her thanks. As a result of visiting the V&A, she had developed a passion for old artifacts and created a business buying and selling antiques. This story reminds me that if we act from the best place in our hearts, we can let go of the need for life to fit in with our own idea of what's right. We can allow life to surprise us.

When I was in my early thirties and engaged in personal development work, I had this belief that if only I solved my problems, then I would be free and happy. So,

I strived ever harder to "clean out my system" from feelings of humiliation, rejection, neediness … and the list went on and on. I recognize this tendency in many other people. As I have gotten older, I have come to realize that we carry these scars with us all of our lives. These pain points are like fault lines in the earth. They may lie dormant for a while, but when the earth's crust moves, the result is an earthquake. Instead of trying to rid ourselves of our so-called problems, we can learn to recognize them as bells of mindfulness and take good care of them. They are like our children, and when they show up hurt, we embrace them and offer our tenderness. We all suffer.

BROTHER PHAP HUU: Ripening moment by moment allows us to relax. Some practitioners come to Plum Village for just one week with high expectations of what they will achieve during this time. If all of their suffering has not been transformed by the end of the retreat, they may feel that it "didn't work" or that they failed. The insight of ripening allows us to understand that the path of practice is a wonderful journey; it takes time and space for things to mature, to transform, and heal.

We may like to think of a tree. It takes time for the seed to be planted; for the roots to deepen; for the tree to grow; for the leaves, flowers, and fruit to appear; and for that fruit to ripen.

Likewise, our practice is a journey of ripening. When we first begin meditating, we're likely to feel very agitated, and we may not enjoy our sitting. That was certainly my experience of sitting meditation for the first four years of practice! In fact, of all the practices in Plum Village, I found seated meditation to be the most difficult. At that time, I felt a need to be very "productive," and sitting still wasn't fulfilling that need. As my understanding deepened and my sitting practice matured—as it ripened—my sitting became the one place where I could let go of my thinking, look deeply at my present moment, and feel the here and now.

Letting Go of the
Need to Be in Control

JO CONFINO: The teaching of ripening helps us understand that everything is always in a process of transformation, which may allow us to relax. The opposite approach to life—the need to control—has many negative impacts. Where does the need to control come from? Because we think we must protect ourselves, often because of past hurts, we may want to position ourselves to avoid ever feeling pain again. Even if we are not aware of it, many of us go through life armored up and constantly alert, our radar scanning the horizon for dangers and already predicting how we will respond if a threat materializes. This hypervigilance is a heavy burden to carry, not only for ourselves but for everyone around us. The compulsion to control makes us inflexible and even brittle.

And yet, there is another, wiser part of ourselves that knows life is far too complex and mysterious to try to manage as we see fit. The more we try to be in control, the less likely it is that we will be open to new possibilities. One of my favorite sayings comes from the Sufi tradition: "Trust in God but don't forget to tie up your camel." This points to the importance of finding the balance of forces in our lives. While we need to consciously act, we can also benefit from flowing with life and trusting our intuition. Even when part of our mind screams at us to act in a certain way, we can take time to listen deeply in order to hear the quieter voice inside that may be offering an alternative path.

There is a classic scene in the film *Star Wars: A New Hope*, in which the hero Luke Skywalker is in a fighter jet seeking to destroy a vast moon-sized battle station created by the "evil" empire to destroy any opposition to its tyranny. Skywalker is trying to fire a torpedo into a tiny vent—the only weak point in the Death Star—to hit the power core and trigger a catastrophic explosion. In his first efforts, he is so clenched that he misses the target. As he is setting up his last attempt, he hears the voice of his mentor Obi-Wan in his head telling him to "Use the force." Luke switches off the navigation system and trusts his instincts to guide the torpedo where it needs to go. And lo and behold, he succeeds. We can do the same, and not only in an emergency situation. When faced with any challenge, it can be wise not to act from fear or anger, but to stop, breathe, and listen to our inner knowing.

Real Community and Belonging

JO CONFINO: Thay famously said that we are living in an age where one Buddha is not enough. One Buddha is not enough to help deal with the many challenges facing the world. We need many Buddhas.

Overwhelm often comes from the idea that we have to do things on our own. Actually, we know that we can be far more effective when we join forces with others. What I see constantly here in Plum Village is the power of community living and the limitation of the current Western view that we are separate individuals best served by building walls to protect ourselves from others. When we see the world from this narrow isolationist perspective, it's much easier to feel overwhelmed. But when we have a community of practice and a community of people, we can feel supported and develop the capacity to support others.

One lesson I was taught as a young man, which has consistently proved to be true over the years, is that when I am facing a difficult challenge, one of the most effective ways to get through the crisis is to reach out to support someone else who is suffering. Why is this the case? When we reach out our hand in friendship, we gain perspective on our own problems, and by being generous to another person who is suffering, we develop our sense of agency. Beyond this, when we see another person benefit from our kindness, it helps open our heart to ourselves. This shift to a more community-focused approach to life can change the whole nature of our experience from one of loneliness, isolation, and suffering to true connection, closeness, and support.

Thay said his greatest achievement lay not in writing more than a hundred books, nor in his ability to convey the Buddha's teachings in a simple and profound way, but in the communities of monastics and laypeople he helped build, which are known as *Sangha*s. He recognized that it is very hard to develop our mindfulness practice if we do not have others to practice with.

"When we practice alone, the energy of mindfulness and concentration we generate may still be weak. It is not yet strong enough for us to transform and bring more space to our heart," Thich Nhat Hanh says. "When we come to a Sangha where many know how to practice and how to generate the energy of mindfulness and concentration, we will see that this is a powerful source of energy. We can borrow from it to do the work of transformation that we alone cannot do. A drop of water flowing toward the sea knows that it can hardly succeed alone.

It could evaporate halfway, become a cloud, wander here and there, and never reach the sea. But if that drop of water enters a river and allows the river to embrace and transform it, then for sure it will arrive at the sea. As practitioners we must allow the Sangha to lead, embrace, and carry us, for us to succeed."

To experience community practice in the Plum Village tradition, there are more than 1,000 physical and virtual Sanghas spread around the world where people meet regularly to practice mindfulness and to share their sufferings and their joys. When we are feeling overwhelmed and overburdened, we can reach out to one of these Sanghas and feel the support of the entire community, a living organism much larger than just ourselves alone.

Impermanence

JO CONFINO: Understanding the core Buddhist teachings on impermanence is another way to stay in balance even when life is swirling around us. When we stop running and look deeply at our situation, we realize that everything is in constant motion. Our cells are dying and being reborn; the weather is constantly in movement; and our feelings and emotions are not the same from one moment to another. It is said we never enter the same river twice, and we are not the same person when we enter the river for the second time. In fact, nothing is going to last forever; even planet Earth will be destroyed in around five billion years when the sun balloons into a giant red star and engulfs this planet.

When I am overwhelmed, in that moment it seems the feeling is going to last forever and that there is no escape. When our lives fill up with so much stuff to do, we may look at it all and say, "Wow, I can't cope." When we're that full, it feels like there's no room left for anything else; even adding one tiny thing more would be the straw that breaks the camel's back. From an intellectual standpoint, we know that this feeling of overwhelm at some point will dissipate, whether it takes a few hours or a few days. But when we are in the thick of it, our emotions often can overwhelm our sense of perspective. The question is, how do we link the knowledge of impermanence to busyness, overwhelm, and the feeling of "Oh my God, I can't cope"?

BROTHER PHAP HUU: Everything is of the nature of impermanence. Our emotions are impermanent; feelings come and go. Some feelings may stay much longer than others, but they also have the nature of impermanence. There's a cycle to it.

Our teacher advised us many times that a strong emotion is like a big storm. We should learn to close the doors of our senses so that the wind doesn't come in and blow everything around. We should learn to close the mind, if only temporarily, to sources of turmoil outside: what we're hearing, what we're listening to, and what is agitating us from the outside. Come back and be with the storm inside. You can witness the hurricane outside, but you are safe in this refuge.

I was a teenager when I first came to Plum Village, before I decided to become a monk, and I often heard Thay give a teaching to the young people on retreat about developing deep belly breathing as an anchor. He told us to put our hands on our abdomen, become aware of the movement of our bellies as we breathe in, and invite our breath to become deeper and slower as we breathe out. This practice of deep breathing has been a true friend to me, one that I always come back to when strong emotions manifest, because it allows me to see the storm without becoming its victim. This is important: especially when we have very strong emotions, we have to remember not to become a victim of them. The emotions are just a part of us; they are not everything we are. An emotion will arise and it will also go away. When you experience intense emotions and feelings, come back to your deep belly breathing and breathe with them. Let the emotion be guided by your breathing.

Having the insight of impermanence, knowing that suffering will end, is helpful. But I also must help to create the conditions for that suffering to end. I need clarity to see how I may be continuing to feed the storm within myself. With deep breathing, I can generate stability, and from this vantage point, I can see deeply into the storm and gain insights into its origin.

Don't wait until you get deep into overwhelm to practice—at that point, it's too late. We have to practice now, when we are clear-headed and well enough in body and mind. When we have energy, we invest in our true nature, our refuge, so that when the time comes and we need that safe space, we can rely on it. Even when you're feeling happy, joyful, or full of love, go back to your refuge. The wholesome feelings of happiness, joy, and love will feed your sense of refuge and help it grow stronger. Your refuge needs nourishment, so please see it as a companion, something to settle into at any moment, and not just as a life jacket in stormy times.

PRACTICE
Stop and Lay Down Your Burdens

BROTHER PHAP HUU: Here is a brief meditation that can help us to come back to our center.

Dear friend, give yourself space to just be still.

If you are standing, feel your two feet on the ground. If sitting or lying down, feel the contact of your body on the ground.

Now, invite yourself to become aware of your in-breath.

As you breathe in, just say, "This is my in-breath."

As you breathe out, just say, "This is my out-breath."

Breathe in and out.

As I breathe in, I allow my breath to become deeper, feeling my abdomen rising. As I breathe out, I allow my breath to settle lower in my body, feeling my abdomen falling. If it is helpful, place the palms of your hands on your abdomen. Or you may like to put one hand on your chest over your heart and one hand on your belly and sense the movement of your breathing in your body.

Deep in-breath. Slow out-breath.

As I breathe in, I recognize calm in me.

As I breathe out, I breathe out with ease.

In, calm. Out, ease.

Breathing in, I offer a smile to myself.

Breathing out, I release everything in my mind, all my worries, the tension.

For this moment, I'm just releasing tension. I smile to myself breathing in and I release, I release my burdens.

Offer a smile of love and tenderness to yourself. Release your fear in this moment, knowing that you are a source of love and compassion.

Breathing in, this is a present moment that I allow myself to dwell in.

Breathing out, this is a wonderful moment.

Being alive, being here.

Because you are alive, everything is possible.

PART 2

Healthy Boundaries

JO CONFINO: In Part I, we focused on the condition of busyness that pervades all aspects of life, highlighting how one person's busyness cannot help but spread busyness to others, just like a stone thrown into a pond sends ripples in all directions. Our society is like a pond into which countless stones are being thrown all at once. How can we respond?

One of the clearest ways to prevent overwhelm and burnout is to create healthy boundaries. If we are not able to assert our needs in a healthy way, we can quickly build up stress in our system as demands arrive from many directions. To cope with this stress, we often withdraw completely or end up attacking those we perceive to be causing us harm —our autonomic nervous system gets triggered into a fight-or-flight response.

Sometimes there is a fine line between being open, vulnerable, and generous and being taken advantage of or falling victim to a situation. It is a line we continually need to navigate. It's similar to a boat threading its way through a narrow channel of water and needing to avoid the sharp rocks that could pierce the hull and bring disaster. The crew needs to be able to see to the horizon while also taking soundings of the water's depth and keeping a keen eye out for danger right in front of them.

We see this dilemma in all areas of life. In Plum Village, I once heard a schoolteacher sharing about the difficulty that he experienced in finding a balance between wanting to be kind and compassionate with his students and needing to be direct and assertive when issues arose. This balancing act is something I personally struggle with, and many of my coaching clients also find this a tough problem to work out. I tend to be conflict-averse, which means that if I am caught in a hard situation, my automatic response is to try to smooth things over and make it OK. The last thing I want to do is start a war. But the impact of continually making things OK for others is that sometimes I end up swallowing my emotions and I'm left with a bad taste in my mouth. On one level, this approach works: the matter has superficially been solved and the other person can go away feeling vindicated. But this approach can leave me feeling unresolved, realizing that I have just created more suffering for myself.

I know that this reaction tends to come from an old pattern of feeling unlovable, which leads me to believe that the most important thing is to fit in, please people, and avoid the risk of being excluded at all costs. Changing this old pattern continues to be a real practice for me on multiple levels: a practice of directly facing whatever issue I have pushed under and allowed to fester, which will have become more difficult to resolve after having been ignored. Turning my attention toward my habitual patterns and changing them by setting boundaries is a practice of self-compassion.

Two Faces of Compassion

BROTHER PHAP HUU: When we practice awareness, first of all we have to come back to ourselves; when we do so, we understand ourselves better. We can recognize that deep within us we contain all the seeds of human experience: we have the seeds of love, compassion, and gratitude as well as the seeds of anger, jealousy, and regret.

When we water the seed of compassion during communication with another human being, our compassion embraces both parties. If compassion comes up during a difficult conversation, our heart expands, and we generate a clearer understanding of the situation. Compassion allows us to be more tender—so we can see the other person and their suffering as more than what they're saying or doing at that moment. Our view becomes wider and clearer: we see that the other person has a backstory, reasons why they suffer, and reasons why they are behaving or speaking in certain unskillful ways. In this way, compassion allows us to accept each other more fully; with compassion in our hearts, we see that each of us suffers and encounters hardships in life.

Alongside compassion, we also have seeds of clarity and firmness; we have a warrior within us, an energy that allows us to be very clear and direct. With this kind of energy, our understanding can be used as a sword that helps cut through illusion.

If you go to a traditional temple in Asia, you will see two protectors dressed like warriors and wearing armor at many temple gates. One protector will look like a very kind *bodhisattva* with a smile of compassion on their face, even though they are carrying a sword. On the other side, there's another protector in the form of a fierce demon, a being who is able to generate fear in others. Like the smiling protector, this demon is also a bodhisattva.

The monastic artists of Mahayana Buddhism created these images to represent two different bodhisattva elements we can generate in ourselves. We should always come back to ourselves—to our body, our feelings, our mind—to know which energy is most skillful for us to allow to surface. If we're interacting with a difficult person, we must ask ourselves, "How much freshness, compassion, and kindness can I cultivate for this person in this moment? How much stability do I have to offer?" We shouldn't feel despair or lose faith in ourselves if we aren't yet able to embrace a difficult situation with compassion. Instead, we should aspire to strengthen our capacity for compassion, our capacity to embrace and transform difficulties through deep presence and communication. In that moment, perhaps it is most skillful to clearly and firmly state our need for space. We are a living organism, so our capacity for love, compassion, and stability is organic; it's a living energy, and it can grow.

Saying No Is a Mantra

BROTHER PHAP HUU: We must be truthful with ourselves about our capacity, and sometimes that means saying "no." Maybe we aren't capable yet of being present in certain difficult situations. In our Zen practice, sometimes saying no is a mantra that teaches us to identify our habits and our state of mind.

One aspect of the Noble Eightfold Path, the Buddha's practical instructions on how to end suffering,* is Right Diligence. The diligence, or effort, we apply here means being mindful of which seeds we water in our daily life. We can ask ourselves, "Am I watering the seeds of mindfulness, the seeds of concentration, the seeds of understanding, and the seeds of kindness? Or am I watering the seeds of violence, anger, fear, anxiety, despair, and jealousy?

---

* The Noble Eightfold Path comprises Right View, Right Thinking, Right Mindfulness, Right Speech, Right Action, Right Diligence, Right Concentration, and Right Livelihood. For more information, see Thich Nhat Hanh, *The Heart of the Buddha's Teaching* (Broadway Books, 1998).

As practitioners, our mindfulness becomes a light to identify what is entering us through our senses: our eyes, our ears, our nose, our tongue, our mind, and our body. We must learn to be mindful of what enters in, because these inputs will water certain seeds in us, affecting the type of energy we can offer to others and our capacity to be present or not for difficult situations. How and what we consume directly influences our capacity to be in a situation with stability and compassion. We can ask ourselves, "Am I consuming in a way that waters the wholesome or unwholesome seeds in me?"

JO CONFINO: We need to say "no" sometimes. If we follow a spiritual path, we might think we always need to be kind and compassionate, to say "yes," to please or pacify others. But we all experience situations in life where we have to put our boundaries firmly in place so as not to get abused. We may need to tell someone to stop what they are doing or escape from a situation that is harmful to our physical or mental well-being. A firm, clear "no" can express true compassion for ourselves and others.

I often see two extreme responses to challenging circumstances: using kindness to hide our feelings in a challenging situation or using aggression and denial as a shield to protect ourselves from truly feeling our pain and suffering. Neither of these extremes leads to a healthy outcome. Both are ways to try not to feel our feelings.

That is why it is important to find what in Buddhism is referred to as the Middle Way, and this applies whether we are tending to our own or someone else's suffering.

My personal experience of the Middle Way is of finding the balance between different forces. I often use the metaphor of a seesaw in a childrens' playground. If we only experience compassion, we are stuck at one end, and if we only experience anger, then we are also stuck. It's as if we're sitting at one end of the plank of wood with no one on the other side. There'll be no movement at all. But by being able to better understand both emotions, we can find our way to the fulcrum, the pivot on which the plank of wood balances, which is always steady. Though our emotions are constantly changing and going up and down, we can be the fulcrum.

Bitter Melon Soup

BROTHER PHAP HUU: A good teacher, leader, parent, or mentor is someone who is attentive to the kind of guidance their student, team, child, or mentee needs. Our teacher, Thay, was very mindful in understanding his students; he was able to see each student differently and recognize what kind of medicine they needed. Positive affirmations were very good for some novice monks because they lifted their confidence. But for others, this same approach could lead to excessive pride or arrogance, which would cause suffering. In those situations, Thay had to dish out the verbal equivalent of the "Zen stick," the thwack with the wooden rod traditionally used during meditation to bring alertness back to a monk suffering from a lapse in concentration.

When Thay offered this kind of very direct teaching, it could sometimes sound quite harsh. But as one of Thay's attendants, I was able to bear witness to more than a handful of these "Zen stick" teachings offered to brothers, sisters, and even to myself. I was able to recognize that whatever form Thay's teaching took, the foundation of it was always love and true understanding. Thay recognized the suffering in us, and his teachings were always an expression of his care. Even when Thay's feedback was tough, his intention was to help us grow, to see our shortcomings. I knew that Thay's ability to teach like this came from his own experience of moving through and learning from many tough situations.

In Vietnam, there's a saying that if you love someone, sometimes you have to give them bitter soup. Like Thay's more direct teachings, not all love is sweet on the surface. At the same time, when we're offering a difficult lesson, we have to be very skillful in our speech and aware of differences. The foundation of our sharing must be one of understanding and love. Whenever Thay gave someone instructions, I saw that he first prepared himself by listening deeply and understanding the situation before offering loving speech.

Loving speech doesn't mean just listing off compliments. There is a way to share about a friend's shortcomings in a loving way so that it can be enlightening to them; we help them to see their mud, but we don't do it from a place of judgment or condescension. Criticizing and complaining are certainly easy habits to fall into in relationships, but they can be destructive. If the other person only hears complaints from us like, "You failed," "You have a problem," "Why do you behave like that?" or "You let me down," they may drown in despair. Particularly if we are in a position of power as a teacher, leader, parent, or mentor, we have to be very mindful of how we speak and act because of the role we represent in the minds of others, the influence we might have over their emotional well-being.

If we are not used to giving bitter soup, we may like to practice with small steps. Loving speech can come in the form of gently helping someone to be aware of something that's upsetting you, something that they're doing unconsciously. To take a small example, we train in Plum Village to be mindful even of ordinary every-day actions such as opening and closing the door when others are meditating. When people first arrive and are still getting used to monastery life, they may not realize how much noise they make when entering or leaving the meditation hall. "My dear friend," I sometimes have to say, "when you open the door in that way, you disturb all of us. Can you be more mindful, more gentle? Please be aware that many of us are already in sitting medita-tion." There's always a tender way to say something very directly and with kindness, allowing the other person to receive your request and act on it. In the end, it's always kinder to them and to yourself to ask for the change you'd like to see happen.

Kindness can be very straightforward. When some-body sees a fault or a weakness in me and they don't tell me directly, or they beat around the bush and make me guess what they're trying to say, that feels unkind. It can feel like they see something unwholesome in me, but they don't yet have the courage to say what it is. I would rather have some bitter melon soup.

As someone who is frequently offering and receiving guidance, I like to reflect: How can I best offer feedback to others in a straightforward way? And how can I practice equanimity with feedback that I myself receive?

Courageous Communication

JO CONFINO: Honest, courageous communication is vitally important because what can appear to be kind on the surface may in fact cause deep suffering. When I first joined the *Guardian* newspaper, I ran the day-to-day operations within the business and finance section, and one of the specialist journalists in my team was suffering deeply. The senior editors of the paper didn't think he was a great journalist, so every time a big story broke in his area of expertise, they gave it to someone else outside of our department to write. For this journalist, it was devastating to be excluded in this way, time after time. Over the years, he suffered increasingly from anxiety and depression because no one ever had the courage to communicate with him about why they made these decisions or to offer him feedback on how he could do better. Instead, they basically ignored and isolated him. I also acknowledge my part in—because even as I worked with him personally to ease his concerns, I did not have the courage to speak out and explain my colleague's pain to the most senior editors.

One could argue that these editors were being kind by not addressing my colleague's shortcomings. But in reality, this behavior was cruel—there was a lack of honesty. The editors didn't have the courage or duty of care to sit down with this person and share their truth. Watching this process unfold changed my life and my perspective on compassion.

When I became a senior editor at the *Guardian*, I made a commitment to do something about this kind of behavior. Journalists are very busy and are often under intense pressure to meet tight deadlines, exacerbated by the need to compete with other media platforms covering the same stories. But these difficult conditions were also repeatedly used as an excuse for why journalists' well-being wasn't cared for—there was no time. Further, while journalists like to tell everyone else what they are doing wrong, they tend not to like to be told the same themselves; they often have fragile egos.

Since there was no time to offer feedback, and no real desire to receive it, there was an element of collusion among the editors, with some journalists not receiving any feedback on their performance for years. As would be expected, fear and deep feelings of isolation festered under a collegiate surface. By introducing a clear process of appraisals, I was able to help to break that cycle and ensure that every journalist had a conversation at least once a year with their boss.

What I learned from my time at the *Guardian* is that if something is not working in our lives, it is much better to be honest about it. If we are in a position of power at work and someone is just not up to the job, it is kinder to face this truth and deal with it head-on. If we feel that someone is failing, chances are they feel it too, and they may therefore also feel lost, afraid, and unsure about how to respond.

Transforming Toxic Feedback
with a Mirror of Mindfulness

BROTHER PHAP HUU: A very dear sister of mine shared her experience of receiving feedback in a toxic workplace. One of her senior colleagues felt it was acceptable to come into the office every day and complain about everyone's performance—including hers—first thing in the morning. By criticizing her and the other junior members of the team, he was directing his frustrations at those with less power, who did not yet have a voice. Most of the time, his colleagues did nothing, pretending to ignore him and passively allowing this unpleasant habit to continue.

One day my friend went into work after having just come back from a retreat at Plum Village, where she had experienced the transformative power of deep listening. She decided that she was going to just look at her senior colleague and really listen to him for the first time and see what would happen. As usual, he came into the office and began criticizing her. She turned her chair and looked directly at him, giving him her full attention. He was stunned. He stopped and said, "Why are you looking at me like that?" She replied, "Well, I want to hear what you have to say." It was a pivotal moment. He stopped bullying her, and eventually other people, after that.

Through her practice of mindful awareness, my friend realized that her colleague was a lonely person. Nobody in his life had listened to him, and therefore these strong emotions of pain and emptiness inside of him expressed themselves through harsh words directed at his workmates. But suddenly, when she listened to him, she became a mirror of mindful awareness for him, in which he saw himself for the first time. Her mindfulness allowed him to recognize and transform his toxic behavior.

My dear sister shared with me that it was a very difficult practice, but when she did it, she saw the power of presence and the courage that we can develop in our interactions. She had to grow and develop a readiness for that moment when she finally set a boundary: "Enough. All right, today I'm just going to look at him and listen." That encounter changed both of them, and they built a new relationship. This transformation occurred through the quality of my friend's presence, not her words.

Therefore, when I have to set boundaries, I always return to myself first. I check in with myself: "What is my energy like right now? Can I cultivate enough deep presence in myself just to listen?" If I don't have the capacity to listen, or the moment is feeling hostile, or not safe enough, it's most important to recognize this and protect ourselves—and that also takes courage.

Protecting Ourselves
from Toxicity and Abuse

JO CONFINO: People can mistake compassion and deep listening with appeasement, and that is why clear boundaries are so important. When we are suffering as a result of another person's behavior, we can fall into the trap of only seeing the other person's pain and ignoring its effect on us, especially if we are people with a high degree of empathy for others. We may find ourselves minimizing or justifying another person's unwholesome actions. For example, we might think, "Well, this person's behavior is very abusive, but actually, I know they came from a very difficult family and I know they're projecting that onto me. If I'm just more kind, more compassionate, and more understanding, if I'm just present with them, then I can change the situation."

But sometimes we can't change the situation. Sometimes a person is acting abusively and dangerously, and we need to vacate that space. We can't be a clear mirror of mindfulness for someone else if our own feelings of calm and trust have been shattered. So, it is important to use our common sense, know when our boundaries are being breached, and to be able to say, "I've done my best, but now for my protection, I need to end this relationship." The Buddha himself recognized this need for boundaries and he taught about the need to protect ourselves.

BROTHER PHAP HUU: Once the Buddha became a teacher, he had to learn a lot about generating boundaries. *Old Path White Clouds* is one of my favorite books by Thich Nhat Hanh. It's the life story of the Buddha, and Thay wrote it in part to remind us that the Buddha was a very human being. Some people have deified the Buddha, but that's the very opposite of how the Buddha himself wanted to be seen—as a human being, as a teacher able to truly transform his suffering. As a monastic studying the history of Buddhism and Zen, when I read *Old Path White Clouds* for the first time, it gave me a glimpse into the growth and development of the Buddha as a great teacher.

The Buddha often presented his teachings in the form of stories, and one is about a wild horse. Having students is like learning to tame wild horses. From time to time, a trainer will meet an untrainable horse, and so the trainer must think about how this one horse, if left untamed in the community, can have an impact on all the other horses. Sometimes the trainer has to recognize the truth of the situation—that this one horse can impact the community negatively—and be willing to return that horse to the wild. Even though the trainer might think they have failed by letting the horse go, this moment of deep looking is an act of compassion for all of the other horses in the trainer's care.

This story illustrates an important point: sometimes we think that after a certain degree of enlightenment, perhaps after becoming a renowned teacher, we are perfect. We may believe we have the capacity to transform everything, to take care of and heal everyone. But that's not how it works—we will always meet people who are not ready to receive the teachings into their hearts. In these cases, bringing mindfulness to the situation, we become aware of our collective energy, capacity, and understanding, and we ask: "How is that person affecting all of us here?"

As an abbot, I have to take this question very seriously. I have to be mindful of harmony in the monastery, of everyone's happiness. Before I was an abbot, when I was Thay's attendant, we once had to ask a monastic to leave the community. It was very difficult, but it was the right thing to do; that monk's pride and ego were so ingrained that he continually challenged Sangha members—even Thay. Thay told me, "Your younger brother came and he asked Thay a question as a challenge. I think the brothers need to have a deep listening session with him to understand what he's going through."

After Thay said this, we spent a long time listening to this brother, unpacking his thoughts, and asking him why he was challenging his monastic brothers and Thay's teachings. After some months, we learned that he had a strong superiority complex; he felt he was there to save the community. One time, I asked him, "What are you trying to save us from? Yes, we suffer, and none of us is perfect, but we're all doing our best to transform. And you're so young, brother, you've been here for less than two years. I think you would benefit from being humbler." He listened, but he didn't want to change, and as more months passed, it was clear that things were not working out. Looking back, I should have been braver; I should have spoken up earlier to the community about my concerns. But because I was close to this brother—we were the same age and there was a sense of companionship—I didn't.

There was a point in our time as monastics growing up together when I felt my brother and I had become quite distant. One afternoon, we were having tea together, and he began to challenge me during our conversation. At one point he splashed tea in my face just to see my reaction. I was quite shocked, but, feeling protected by a strong energy of compassion, I didn't do anything. Even so, I was able to recognize that a boundary had been crossed and it was time to stop. "Okay," I said, "our conversation is over. I think our tea ends here." I could feel the energies of hurt, anger, and violence manifesting within me in reaction to his disrespectful behavior, but

I was able to use my practice of mindfulness to quickly become aware of my own energy and remove myself from his presence. At the time, I didn't tell anyone about this encounter because, despite everything, I wanted to protect his reputation.

About three months after this incident, this brother's behavior was an agenda item at our main community meeting. All of us realized we were at our limits. So, we went to Thay and said, "Thay, the monastic sangha would like to ask this brother to leave. We feel like we don't have the capacity to embrace his suffering and maybe our level of understanding is not great enough to help him transform it." And Thay agreed that we had to let him go.

After telling the brother that he had to leave, he felt a lot of sorrow, regret, and grief—and so did I. There was a sense of loss. Looking back, I sometimes wonder if I had been able to share about that most painful moment—when he splashed me with tea—at the time it happened, maybe we could have had more support and direct guidance about how to handle the situation; maybe we could have practiced more deep listening to help him identify the source of his anger and stop it from growing. Perhaps the outcome could have been different. I don't want to dwell on that situation, but it taught me two valuable lessons: the importance of speaking up in a timely way and also how to "let go of a wild horse" when the community's harmony is in jeopardy.

The Attack-Back Syndrome

JO CONFINO: When we are feeling stressed or overwhelmed, we often see situations only from our side of the story because we tend to go into survival mode. While I may be certain that someone is crossing my boundaries, they may equally believe that I am crossing theirs—there are two sides to every conflict. In a situation like this, it may be that both of us are experiencing a sense of hurt or injustice and that both of us firmly believe we are right and the other is wrong. This often leads to defensiveness, anger, and then the wish to counterattack. The violence can escalate as we are swept away by our emotions and carried a long way from our center. It's even harder to find a solution when pride interferes, and neither party wants to appear weak by stepping back into the center. We see this in the many wars and conflicts between nations but also in our own families and communities.

BROTHER PHAP HUU: When this strong energy flares up, you must first come back to your mindfulness of anger. Don't push it away, don't say "I'm not angry." Don't deny it. Instead, you can say to yourself, "I'm angry, but I want to be mindful of this energy and I want to take care of it."

If you have to address the situation right away, speak slowly and be intentional about your choice of words. Acknowledge your feelings. You can say, "I feel hurt, my dear colleagues, I hear what you've said, and I feel misunderstood. But I want to understand why you have that perception. Can you share more so I can understand why you think of me like that or why my view has been pushed aside? And afterward, can you allow me time to also express my point of view?" This is an example of how to speak so that we acknowledge others. I think when somebody attacks us, it's because they feel unacknowledged—unheard and unseen. Therefore, their tone of voice carries the energy of rejection and anger. It's like a baby crying, just asking to be heard.

To defuse a situation like this is not to be passive; it's a means of protection. We don't want to be violent toward ourselves, so we need to give ourselves some space. We can even say, "My dear friends, I'm very emotional right now and I'm choosing not to respond, to allow myself time to take care of my feelings so I can speak more positively. I want to respond when I'm in a more peaceful state. I want to embrace and take care of my anger right now."

It is a strength to be able to set a boundary around anger so it doesn't burn you or the other person. Saying something like this can also offer the other person an opportunity to recognize their emotions and take care of them. In this way, we each become more responsible for ourselves, while recognizing that everything we do affects one another.

Beginning Anew

JO CONFINO: Thay developed a powerful practice, which he called Beginning Anew, to help build harmonious relationships and the capacity to deal with difficulties when they arise. At the heart of Beginning Anew are two other core Plum Village practices: deep listening and mindful speech. Because we express what we need from the other person clearly and lovingly through this practice, Beginning Anew is an active way to create healthy boundaries. I know this from direct experience: as I have been practicing Beginning Anew with my wife, Paz, nearly every week since the very start of our relationship eighteen years ago.

Paz wisely says that even though we enjoyed a magical start to our relationship, our love needs regular maintenance in order to stay fresh. Thay used the metaphor of stalagmites and stalactites in a cave to illustrate how a relationship can deteriorate. Each drip of water coming through the cave ceiling looks innocent enough but leaves a tiny deposit of minerals, and repeated over and over again, these minuscule droplets eventually form a calcified monolith.

If we don't pay attention to the small irritations that come up in any relationship, we can look back one day to realize that they have created a mountain of anger and resentment. In fact, the feelings of overwhelm and burn-out often arise after many small issues come up together to create a powerful emotional storm. If we deal with a situation earlier, we may be able to prevent things from getting out of control.

There are four stages to the formal practice of Beginning Anew, and each person goes through the whole process before the other person takes their turn. During the first stage, called flower watering, we express the specific qualities we really appreciate in the other person. With Paz, for example, I would not say something general like "You're so generous"; instead, I might point out how she had taken care of all the cooking that week because she knew I was busy and wanted to support me. The second stage of Beginning Anew is to express any regrets we may have around something we said or did. For example, I might apologize for having been short-tempered in response to her request for something when I was already busy. The purpose of these first two stages is to acknowledge the other person's many positive qualities and to admit that we ourselves are not perfect.

With these two steps, we have already taken the sting out of the third part of the process, which is expressing a hurt that we've experienced. It is crucial not to use blaming language such as "You did this" or "You said that," but to take responsibility for my own emotions while also helping the other person to recognize where he or she may have been unskillful. For example, I might say to Paz that I felt unappreciated after spending hours fixing something for her in her art studio and not receiving any acknowledgment in return.

The fourth, final, and sometimes most difficult step of Beginning Anew is asking for help. For many of us, it is tough to admit there is something we cannot handle on our own. While we may be very willing to offer help to someone else in need, it can be hard to call in support for ourselves. Practicing the fourth step could look something like: "I am struggling to get the language right for this book on overwhelm. Can you please read this section and offer me some suggestions?" After this last stage, we swap places and move through the steps again. Normally, we end with a hug and express our appreciation for being able to share this life together.

PRACTICE
Beginning Anew

Dear friend, find time and space to sit with your partner or friend to begin anew.

1. Flower watering: express your appreciation.
2. Express a regret.
3. Express a hurt, without attaching blame and speaking in the first person. ("I felt ....")
4. Ask for help.

Exchange places and repeat the steps.

End the practice with appreciation for one another.

The beauty of this practice is that it can be done with anyone, including work colleagues or even in teams. If the other person does not have a spiritual practice, it can be off-putting for them to hear that you want to sit down and do a formal Beginning Anew session. Instead, incorporate the essential aspects of the practice into a normal conversation, and recognize that Beginning Anew does not need to include all four stages to be beneficial. If you don't have a regret, for example, don't feel you have to make one up! It is very important, though, to start with flower watering, even if—maybe especially if—you are itching to get to your hurt. If you start off with a complaint, no matter how justified you feel, you are only throwing fuel on the fire. Someone is much more likely to listen to what has upset you when you have first expressed appreciation for them. Of course, it goes without saying that we should not use flower watering just to soften the other person up in order to deliver our knockout punch!

A Bell of Mindfulness in Meetings

BROTHER PHAP HUU: Earlier in this book, we described our practice with the many bells in Plum Village—stopping whatever we are doing and returning to our in-breath and out-breath. After listening to the bell in Plum Village, people sometimes bring the practice of listening to a bell into their workplaces, especially to help regulate the atmosphere in meeting settings. Inviting the bell in meetings gives people a chance to stop, breathe, and come back to themselves. When the energy of conflict builds up around a meeting topic, we all need a moment to come back to ourselves, because if we move ahead and continue to create something on top of a feeling of tension, anxiety, or opposition, I don't think the result could be what we really want.

In Plum Village, we don't want the final decision for anything to be based on anger or a sense of division. A mindful facilitator can orient us toward our intention during meetings and can remind us to be more skillful in our sharing, not to bypass any suffering, but to be considerate and use words that can offer clarity without putting someone down. During a meeting, often we sit in a circle facing one another, and the facilitator sits with the bell. Before we begin to speak, we join our palms together and bow in. During a discussion, if any one of us senses tension arising, the facilitator will invite the sound of the bell, which guides everyone to come back to their breathing. If someone is aware that they have caused disruption, they have an opportunity to acknowledge it, apologize, and begin anew right away to bring the harmony back. In my years as a facilitator, we have had several times when brothers have become aware that their sharing was not coming from a place of balance, so they joined their palms and said, "Dear sangha, I am aware that my sharing was very emotional. I would like to begin anew."

We may think that it's weak to admit to becoming emotional in a meeting, but there is actually such power and courage in sharing our vulnerability—it builds harmony and understanding in the group who is listening. Once, during a high-tension meeting in our community, an elder monastic set a boundary and said, "I would like to advise that we stop our meeting because this kind of disharmony and the tone of voice being used will not lead to the outcome we want. I would like us to stop. Let's come back to our breathing and take care of ourselves, of each and every individual. And let us come back tomorrow with clarity and a more positive energy." And that was exactly the right thing to do. Just by giving us a little bit of space, another sixteen hours, the elder monk gave us the opportunity to come back to ourselves and take care of our emotions. Nothing is lost by taking this time away. If we force ourselves to push through certain difficult meetings, then we may well regret the outcome.

We aspire to practice mindfulness in meetings and make decisions when we are feeling happy, well, and peaceful enough. By holding meetings in a mindful way, it becomes habitual to generate stability, to be aware of our anger rising, and to set boundaries that protect ourselves and our relationships. Thich Nhat Hanh wrote the following meditation for monastic meetings to help create and hold a safe space for discussions.

Meditation before Meetings

We vow to go through this meeting in a spirit of togetherness as we review all ideas and consolidate them to reach a harmonious understanding or consensus.

We vow to use the methods of loving speech and deep listening in order to bring about the success of this meeting as an offering to the Three Jewels [Buddha, Dharma, Sangha].

We vow not to hesitate to share our ideas and insights but also vow not to say anything when the feeling of irritation is present in us.

We are resolutely determined not to allow tension to build up in this meeting. If any one of us senses the ·start of tension, we will stop immediately and practice Beginning Anew right away so as to reestablish an atmosphere of togetherness and harmony."

Please do not wait until you are angry, until you are experiencing difficult emotions, to practice mindfulness. At that moment, it is too late. We must invest in our capacity to embrace ourselves fully and call our emotions by their names in the present moment. Don't think that your happiness isn't a good enough object of mindfulness. You have to be aware of your happiness, the goodness and well-being that are there so that when the ill-being comes around, as it inevitably will, you can embrace it. Don't wait until that moment.

Digging Two Graves

JO CONFINO: The benefit of delaying our response to a hurt is valid in many circumstances. We have probably all heard the classic piece of advice never to respond immediately to difficult email messages. Waiting on emails is a great example of watching our emotions at work. I don't think there's a single email I've kept intact after waiting and reviewing it the following morning before finally sending it off. The emails I've written in the heat of the moment tend either to be accusatory or defensive, and either way they risk making matters worse. If I let myself calm down and be mindful, by the time I reread the message, I invariably see that it is based on a desire to get back at the other person and make them pay a price for the upset they have caused me.

Watching this process of emotional unfolding has taught me a lot about the seed of revenge we carry inside of ourselves. When we feel overwhelmed or in danger of burning out, we may want to deflect from our own painful feelings by painting them onto the person we blame for our predicament—even if that person is dead or otherwise no longer a part of our lives. We want them to suffer.

Several times, I have witnessed people who have repeatedly sabotaged their own lives in order to "prove" their lives have been ruined by the other person. The effect of this is especially acute when the person regularly feeds that energy of blame. Given the choice of being happy or being stuck in a pattern of failure and blame, some people unconsciously continue to think of themselves as a victim as a way of seeking revenge on the person whom they see as the perpetrator of their suffering. In effect, they are saying, "Because of what you did to me, you have ruined my life and I can never be happy"—and then they need to live by that story. If their life is going well, they end up sabotaging their success to maintain their belief system. Wanting revenge very rarely, if ever, eases a situation.

As someone once taught me, if you want revenge, dig two graves. Why two? Because you'll have to dig one for yourself, too. You might think you're digging a grave to bury the other person, but the consequences of your deep anger and blame mean you are also killing yourself. By starting to recognize and let go of our blame and our anger, we can turn toward our happiness and away from our suffering.

The Art of Letting Go

BROTHER PHAP HUU: Throughout our lives, we make many friendships and other types of relationships, but they may not always last. Rather than holding onto our pain when a friendship ends, it is important to develop the art of letting go. We must acknowledge the reality that pushing ourselves to continue certain relationships can be harmful, and we need to learn to let go.

Here's an example. I have a younger brother in the Dharma (someone who ordained as a monk after I did), whom I truly admired and enjoyed being around. He was a very good songwriter, and he wrote many beautiful songs in Vietnamese. At the time we were friends, I was trying to improve my Vietnamese, and I sang his songs as a way of learning the language, as an easy way to expand my vocabulary. One day, seemingly out of the blue, he gave me the cold shoulder and ignored me. It came as a real shock. I started to think, "What did I do wrong to make him angry? What happened yesterday? Did I say something to offend him?" I was also careful to practice the mantra "Are you sure?" to see if this was just a wrong perception on my part. I continued trying to connect with him socially in various settings, but when I entered tea circles, for instance, he would jump up and leave. This was incredibly painful, especially as I was also dealing with my own complexes. At this point, I began to be critical of myself.

But one day, I had a breakthrough, and I accepted things just as they were: I accepted that we were no longer friends and that I might not ever understand what he's going through. I needed to let go. So, I started to love that brother from a distance. When I'd sit for meditation practice, I would send him good wishes, using words like, "Okay, brother, I hope that you have peace, that you have joy, and that you are transforming whatever it is you're going through."

I was bitter toward that brother of mine for a while. I thought, "He pushed me away when I didn't do anything wrong! How dare he have such a negative perception about me!" My bitterness and sense of being wronged began to affect the way I looked at him. I gave the cold shoulder I was receiving from him right back. But when we start to mirror the pain that we receive, we must practice setting our intention to be okay with someone not loving us. We don't have to become that cold shoulder. We don't have to become that hatred. Instead, we continue to cultivate loving kindness in ourselves, because we know we have many other friendships that we can nourish.

Some years have passed and he is now in a different monastery. Whenever I see him, I offer my greetings and I gauge the energy between us. About three years ago, after checking in and realizing he still didn't want to communicate much, I created my own boundary again. In Buddhism, practicing the Middle Way, we know it's good not to be too tight or intense nor to be too loose with situations and relationships; we cultivate a sense of knowing what is enough, when to lean in, and when to back off.

This brother helped me to realize that I didn't have to be so attached to being liked by everyone. I still have relationships with other brothers and sisters, and I am still growing. It's okay to lose one friendship. I know now that it wasn't skillful to drag myself down and expend energy on a relationship that the other person clearly didn't want to build together. At the time, this situation was part of my meditation almost every day. I did a lot of deep looking, I spent a lot of time thinking, "What did I do wrong?" But a moment came when I just let it go. And sometimes true love is just that—learning to let go.

As powerful as it was for me to accept that not everyone would like me, it was equally important to realize that I am also not able to love everyone all the time. But I can continue to cultivate love in myself.

Never Too Late to Make Peace

JO CONFINO: One of the insights from my Plum Village practice is that it is never too late to make peace with someone. If we have said something that has caused hurt, Thay advises us to send a kind thought to catch up with the angry one and neutralize it. How we respond to someone who has passed away is just as valuable as for a person who is still alive.

We think that when someone dies, time stops and it's too late to repair our relationships. What I have learned, though, is that it's never too late. Through our ability to reflect and remember, we can in the present moment go back and heal the past. The remarkable thing is that when we change our perception of the past, this changes our perception in the present. And when we change our perception in the present, we cannot help but change our future.

We can communicate with someone who is no longer in our lives in many different ways. We can talk to them, write a letter to them, and pray for them. We don't need to let the concept of time as a linear process stop us from doing the healing work that can free us from our self-imposed prison of regret and suffering.

My wife, Paz, has a practice that really works for her. If she finds it difficult to reach a resolution with one person, she will offer kindness to someone else, trusting that the energy will also reach the person she is having a difficulty with. One summer in New York, she was having a hard day. A friend in a meditation group she was running had accused her of being unkind. While Paz felt she had been misunderstood, she left the conversation with the seed of doubt that maybe she had been unskillful. As she was walking home on that baking hot day in Manhattan, she saw an unhoused man on the sidewalk with nothing to drink. She went into a shop, bought some water, and gave it to him. In that instant, she burst into tears because she recognized that this act of generosity was also healing the hurt and self-doubt that she had experienced just a few minutes before. Paz's insight was that on the ultimate level, it doesn't really matter what our story is; we are all interconnected and therefore healing can take place in many manifestations. Since then, she has made offering kindness to others a conscious part of her practice.

Interbeing,
No-Self, and Boundaries

JO CONFINO: The example of my wife's kindness to a stranger as a way of healing a different hurt reflects the core Plum Village teaching of *interbeing*, the understanding that we are not separate selves and cannot exist by ourselves alone. Everything is connected. Within each of us is the whole cosmos: our ancestors, nature, stardust, and every person we have ever met. They have all contributed to the way we are. We are made of non-human elements: the sunshine, the rain, the food we eat, and so on. The entire universe contributes to our existence. If we were to remove a single one of these elements, we would cease to be.

I remember listening to Thay talk about mindful eating when I first came to Plum Village. He said that if we were to look deeply into a single piece of carrot on our fork, we would be able to see the entire universe within it. I was skeptical at the time, but when I stopped to look, it was so obviously true—the carrot needs the sun in order to grow, and the whole universe needs to exist for the sun to be present in it.

This understanding of interrelatedness, oneness, and interbeing could appear incompatible with the need for boundaries, which can create a sense of separation. If we feel we need to protect or defend ourselves, that suggests there is a self to protect. This is where the Buddhist understanding of the two dimensions of reality—the historical dimension and the ultimate dimension—becomes very helpful.

BROTHER PHAP HUU: First of all, we have to understand that the teaching of no-self doesn't mean we don't exist. No-self is the insight of interbeing: looking at our own body, we see we are conditioned by so many other things. In the ultimate dimension of reality, there are no boundaries. This is a deep teaching in Buddhism.

But in the historical or relative dimension, meaning our everyday lives, we do have to create rules to help us protect ourselves and be in harmony. One part of the teaching is to touch the ultimate dimension, to generate boundless love and a boundless mind that can see the interbeing nature of everything. But in the historical dimension, we must collectively set healthy boundaries.

To give an example, as monastics, we maintain precepts as helpful boundaries to protect us. Our precepts cover every aspect of life, and many of them help us not to form habits that may not serve us. For example, we may be attracted to drinking, but there is a precept that instructs us not to sit at a bar where there is alcohol, dim light, music, and maybe unwholesome energy. We are training to generate a compassionate heart and a right mind, and if we go into those places, we can easily become tempted and return to old habits. The precepts serve as boundaries to help us maintain our deepest aspiration. They aren't there to push people away, but to help us learn to guard ourselves.

If we fail to create healthy boundaries, we become like the skinless cow in the Buddha's teaching on sensory impressions, unable to protect itself from being eaten alive:

> Suppose there is a cow who has lost most of its hide. When the cow leans against an earthen wall, all the little creatures who inhabit the wall come and eat the flesh of the cow. The same happens when the cow leans against a tree, or if the cow were to step into water, all the little creatures living in the water would come and suck its blood. If the cow were exposed to the air, all the creatures in the air would come and feed off the cow. When you understand the food of sense impression and the three kinds of feelings—pleasant, painful, neutral—correctly, there is nothing more you need to do.

The skinless cow is a metaphor for our mind. If we don't learn to guard our mind, unwholesome elements can infect us. We will become that unwholesome energy.

If we see a suffering person, we can recognize their pain and we can also see that their suffering has causes. If we look more deeply with the understanding of inter-being, we see that their suffering is also our suffering. We can transform that suffering inside of ourselves; for instance, by transforming one of the habits or behaviors that we share with that person. Of course, we don't want to take on that habit for them—we don't take on their suffering. But if we're skillful, we can transform our own habits, and the other person can as a result receive our kindness, our understanding, and our transformation, and this can help them change.

From a Murderer to a Monk

BROTHER PHAP HUU: There's a very famous story of the Buddha's encounter with a serial killer, Angulimala. This man held the wrong view that he needed to kill a thousand people to win the approval of his teacher. And from each person he killed, he took a token of one of their fingers, and he created a necklace out of these fingers and wore it around his neck. That's why his name was Angulimala—in the Pali language, *anguli* means finger and *mala* means necklace.

One day the Buddha was walking in the village where Angulimala was seeking his thousandth victim, and the villagers implored the Buddha to hide from murderer. But the Buddha was a very capable and confident person, a prince who was well-trained in martial arts, and he was on a mission to intercept Angulimala. Angulimala saw the Buddha coming toward him and he said, "Stop, stop Buddha." The Buddha continued walking fearlessly toward him. The Buddha said, "I have already stopped; it is you who have not stopped." This shocked Angulimala; he didn't understand what the Buddha was saying. "What are you talking about? You're the one that's walking, you foolish man." And the Buddha, with authority, said, "I have stopped my wrong actions in this lifetime, but you are continuing to do evil action. You need to learn to stop."

At that moment, Angulimala woke up. Because the Buddha was so fearless and courageous and his presence was so powerful, Angulimala had to listen to him. Angulimala looked back at his actions and fully realized the extent of what he had done. On the spot, Angulimala broke down and started to repent, saying, "Buddha, what do I do now? I have killed people; I have done so much harm. What can I do to atone for these crimes?" And the Buddha said, "In this moment, you have recognized your wrong actions, and it's a moment of rebirth. This is an opportunity for you to change, to practice the way of love and understanding and nonviolence."

Angulimala said, "I want to be your student. I want to be a monk, but I'm afraid I won't be accepted because I have performed so many wrong actions and caused so much harm." The Buddha said, "If you are ready to be hated, if you are ready to still be seen as a killer, but if you are also ready transform in this moment, I will allow you to become my student. People will see you and they will shout at you. People will throw rocks at you because you've done so much harm. But this is also a part of the healing that you need to demonstrate. You need to show that you've changed and are still changing." Angulimala accepted and he received the name Ahimsaka, which means "the harmless one," from the word *ahimsa* or nonviolence.

When Angulimala became a monk, he did have to face hatred directed toward him when he joined the monastics on their alms round. But the Buddha taught him, "Every time somebody throws harsh language and an unkind gaze at you, you have to breathe with awareness and accept it. You have to come back to yourself and generate your compassion and your understanding that you've committed acts that caused suffering. But now, you are beginning anew, and you are changing. In this moment, this action of not reacting will show people that you've changed and are still changing."

One day, the king heard that Angulimala, the notorious bandit and serial killer, had become a monk, and he couldn't believe it. He came to the Buddha and asked, "Did you really ordain him?" And the Buddha said, "Yes, he's right there. There he is, with his hair and beard shaved off, a member of the monastic order." The king was so impressed that he decided not to persecute and punish Angulimala.

The story of Angulimala shows that a person can truly change, but there are conditions that must be present for this change to occur. In this case, the Buddha put up a boundary; he was unwilling to take on Angulimala's suffering. And this boundary was a condition for Angulimala to reflect on his past actions and to transform.

Don't Let Boundaries
Become Barriers

BROTHER PHAP HUU: When we are ready, we can expand our boundaries. When we feel safe and solid enough, and we realize that a boundary is preventing us from growing, we may be able to let it go.

A great example of this is hugging meditation. Traditionally, a Buddhist monk doesn't have physical contact with other people. But Thay explained to us that when he was teaching in the West, one of his lay students whom he met in the United States was so moved and had so much gratitude toward Thay that she didn't know what to do with herself to express that love. Thay was at the airport, leaving to board his plane, and she just came up to him and spontaneously hugged him. Thay said he was awkward and stiff, like a log! Afterward when he was sitting on the flight, he realized that hugging is a Western way of expressing admiration and gratitude. "If I am going to take root in the West and build a community here, I have to open my boundaries a little bit in order to blend and to take root so that others can receive this teaching."

Hugging meditation is to really acknowledge that the other person is there, hugging them while taking three mindful breaths. With the first breath, we just say, " I am here for you." With the second breath, "I know you are there and I'm so happy." And on the third breath, we remember that we are of the nature of impermanence, and that one day we have to let go.

Boundaries can be protective and can support our spiritual practice, but sometimes boundaries become obstacles, and we have to learn to open them. Hugging meditation is an example of how Thay could skillfully open up and practice in a way that best suits the particular historical and cultural moment.

Boundaries Create Space for Our Deeper Aspirations to Manifest

JO CONFINO: We are fortunate that Thay created so many accessible practices. In fact, the reason we created the podcast series *The Way Out Is In* is because we wanted to present the practical and immediate applications of Buddhist teachings. This very much mirrors Thay's aspiration, which is apparent in the Five Mindfulness Trainings—Thay's renaming of the classic Five Precepts shared by all Buddhist traditions—where the word "training" instead of "precept" reminds us that these are not prohibitions but rather commitments to practice.* Crucially, the Five Mindfulness Trainings are Thay's way of expressing a new global ethic, that, when we observe it at an individual and collective level, transforms our world.

The first training is to protect life and decrease violence in oneself, in the family, and in society. The second

---

* For more on the Five Mindfulness Trainings, see *The Mindfulness Survival Kit* (Parallax Press, 2013).

focuses on social justice, generosity, refraining from stealing, and not exploiting other living beings. The third is the practice of responsible sexual behavior. The fourth is the practice of deep listening and loving speech in order to restore communication and reconcile. The fifth concerns mindful consumption to help stop us from poisoning our minds and bodies. These trainings are also boundaries, offering us guardrails of mindfulness that can help us to lead healthier and happier lives and prevent us from feeling overwhelmed or burning out.

The trainings are not hard and fast rules but offer us a path to a more peaceful and compassionate world. This is very important: by describing our practice with the trainings as a path, we recognize that it takes time to change. We acknowledge that if we try to do too much, too soon, we will sabotage our efforts by stimulating the part of our mind that believes we are fine just the way we are and that the wish to change would destabilize us. Equally important is Thay's understanding that, given our wish to feel free, if we see the trainings as rules not to be transgressed, then part of our mind will seek to rebel against this idea of authority. To give an example of this, if we are put under great external pressure to see a counselor or a therapist, then we may well look for a reason why therapy doesn't work by finding fault with the therapist or the modality. But if we conclude that we need some professional help and seek out that support with our own volition, we are likely to gain far more from therapy. Even if the person we choose is not right for us, we are more likely to persevere, learn from our experience, and find someone more suitable.

Referring to the Five Mindfulness Trainings, Thay said: "Mindfulness protects us, our families, and our society. When we are mindful, we can see that by refraining from doing one thing, we can prevent another thing from happening. We arrive at our own unique insight. It is not something imposed on us from an outside authority."

Rather than seeing boundaries as a rigid wall, we can start to see them as a permeable membrane and as the foundation for our aspiration to find more happiness and joy. They show us the possibility of a better future, and they also allow us not to judge ourselves too harshly when we don't fully measure up to our ideals. This is critical because if we fail to meet our own expectations of ourselves and we beat ourselves up, this guilt can drag us back into the very situation we have been trying to escape. If, for example, we commit to stop eating sweet foods but then tuck into a couple of doughnuts, we may experience self-hate, and that may lead us to eat even more cakes and chocolate as an escape from the pain of failure. It is important not to use the spiritual path as an excuse for self-flagellation or to perpetuate a belief we will never be enough.

Setting appropriate boundaries and taking small actions in service to our aspiration is to be kind to ourselves. Just like a child learning to walk, we focus on putting one foot in front of the other without the feeling of needing to run a marathon.

Making Mistakes
Is a Way to Grow

BROTHER PHAP HUU: We can all make mistakes and act in ways that do not represent who we truly are. The secret to happiness is to see that these difficult moments give us a chance to reflect, learn, and become better human beings.

I had a very deep relationship with Thay, and as his attendant, I had the privilege to see him in a way that few other people were able. Thay expressed immense generosity as a teacher and was always willing to learn from his mistakes. I saw him transform through the years. In the early days, Thay was stricter and more direct with us, but as the years passed, I saw him soften and become much more expressive in his compassion—without losing that directness.

Thay continually grew as a teacher and learned from his own way of teaching. He always showed humility, sometimes asking me and other monastics after a public talk: "Do you think the way Thay shared the Dharma with the community today was good enough?" This is a Zen master sincerely and humbly asking his students, who are all beginners, for their feedback. He modeled that openness to allow us also to grow in openness and love.

Thay's capacity to love the difficult people in his life also expanded through the years. For instance, there was a nun who was ordained at the same time as me, and we grew up together as monastics. At one point, she went through a very difficult period in her monastic career, and she was unsure about her direction and whether she should remain a nun. When we ordain, it's a commitment for life, so her doubt was really tearing her apart, and it was causing all of us around her to suffer, too.

Thay spent a great deal of time listening to her and doing his best to help her, but to me it seemed as if she was using up too much of his attention. I was also able to see that it caused sadness in Thay to see his student suffer. I felt her suffering was pushing at the edges of my own boundaries, and my capacity to love her was being tested.

One day, in my naiveness, I went to Thay and said, "Thay, just let her go! I feel like she's taking too much of your energy." And Thay, with the gentlest smile, looked at me and said, "Phap Huu, one day, when you become a teacher, you will understand." The love that Thay had for his students was boundless. He would do everything in his power to help them stay on their chosen path. He said, "When you become a teacher, that student is you. So, I cannot push that student away."

The moment Thay said this has stayed with me—very present, very alive. We were in Thay's hut in Deer Park Monastery in California. I was sitting on his left side, and the tenderness with which Thay turned and looked at me has now become my teaching. That is interbeing.

At that point, Thay had been a teacher for many, many years, and his love had expanded so much that his ability to embrace suffering was profound. Later on, after another five or six years, this sister did leave, but she never forgot the love and understanding that she received from Thay. After she left, she shared with me that she had never received such profound love from anyone, and that this love would never be lost.

Nothing in our experience is lost, and we can never predict the effects of the love we offer to others. And as our heart grows, our capacity to hold the suffering also grows, allowing our boundaries to become less rigid.

Your Presence Changes the World

BROTHER PHAP HUU: You have the power to know yourself. Presence itself is a teacher. What I've learned most from many senior teachers, elders in the community, and from Thay himself, is that our transformation takes place not just by listening to teachers' words but through nonverbal transmission, by allowing their way of being to influence us. For example, when these teachers walk in meditation, it can remind us of our tendency to rush, so by walking with them, we slow down and walk more mindfully, without effort.

Once, when I was feeling very lost and anxious, I saw a brother just walk mindfully along the path in the monastery. And that was the teaching I needed at that moment. Seeing him reminded me not to be carried away by all the negative thoughts that my mind was producing and to come back to the safe island within myself, stopping the tide of my unchecked emotions. It is a healthy boundary not to allow an unwholesome mental formation to color our entire experience of the present moment. We *can* stop our nonstop thinking radio station, embrace our anxiety, and let it be with a different energy. Boundaries are there for us to not lose ourselves in our thoughts, but to center ourselves in our breathing and our presence.

We cannot measure the magnitude of the changes caused by the presence of someone who is taking care of themselves, fully awake and fully mindful. By taking care of ourselves, we change ourselves, our own nervous systems, and, resonating through our communities, the collective systems of life on Earth.

Dharma Rain

In Plum Village, we often talk about "Dharma rain." We don't have to take notes during a talk or try to memorize the teachings, whether they come via the written or spoken word. The teachings are a transmission, not an exercise in intellectual rigor. Whatever is helpful, we integrate into our lives; whatever does not seem to support us in our journey, we release.

Sometimes people on retreat would fall asleep during Thay's talks because they were not used to getting up early for the 6:00 a.m. sitting meditations that preceded his sharing. Thay would say not to wake them and not to ask them to leave the hall—they would benefit from the teachings just by being there, even if their conscious minds were not active at that moment!

Our hope is that you benefit from some of the practices and insights contained within this book and that they support you in having a greater sense of balance, peace, and happiness in your daily life. Buddhist teachings and practices on equanimity, peace of mind, understanding, and love are there to be experimented with in the flow of living, including in the cycle of busyness, overwhelm, burnout, and renewal. We hope the teachings that resonate with you accompany you through life, and if there are some that don't make a positive difference, please let them go for now; stay open to the possibility that they may ripen over time.

We soak up the nutrients we need just like the earth soaks up the rain. And what the ground cannot contain gets washed into the river and down to the sea, which evaporates to create more rain. Nothing is lost.

PRACTICE
Offering Strength and Space to Loved Ones

BROTHER PHAP HUU: Dear friend, wherever you may be, allow yourself a moment to be still.

Allow me to guide you through some mindful breathing.

> First, bring your attention to your in-breath.
> As you breathe in, just call your in-breath by its
>   name. This is the in-breath.
> As you breathe out, call your out-breath by its
>   name. This is the out-breath.
> In, out.
> And as you breathe in, you can feel your in-breath
>   coming in as your abdomen is rising.

And as you breathe out, you can feel your abdo-
  men falling.
Feel your in-breath, and feel your out-breath.
Rising. Falling.
As you breathe in, offer kindness to your body.
As you breathe out, allow yourself to relax.
Relax in your face, your shoulders, your arms,
  your hands, your chest, your back, your but-
  tocks, your two legs, and your two feet.
In-breath, kindness to your body.
Out-breath, I relax.
Breathing in, I take care of my stability, of my
  presence.
Breathing out, I nourish the mountain inside
  of me.
In, stability in presence.
Out, solid as a mountain.
Breathing in, there is space in my heart.
Breathing out, I offer that space to those who
  are close to me, to my loved ones.
In, offering space.
Out, to my loved ones.
Breathing in, with this breath, I feel so alive
  inside of me.
As I breathe out, I connect to life all around me.
In, life inside of me.
Out, life all around me.

Breathing in, this is the present moment.
Breathing out, this is a wonderful moment.
In, present moment.
Out, wonderful moment.

Appreciation

JO CONFINO: Brother Phap Huu once told me the story of being with Thay when a book he had written was delivered to him hot off the press. Rather than any self-congratulation, Thay took the book and placed it on the altar and touched the earth in a full-body prostration. This was to express his thanks to all the spiritual ancestors, blood ancestors, and land ancestors who had passed on their love and wisdom, thereby creating the conditions for that particular book to manifest.

This story touched me deeply because it was a reminder that we never create anything by ourselves alone. Whatever we do is the result of the countless thoughts and actions of others down through the generations who have helped infuse our lives with their wisdom and given us the opportunity to show up. And the time has now come to see the publication of my first book, cowritten with the legendary Brother Phap Huu—an honor and a delight. Thank you, Brother Phap Huu.

Holding this book in my hands, I hope I am also able to see all the non-me elements in it. With all this firmly in my mind, I want to express my appreciation to all the teachers who have given me the strength and insight to walk this path. I see in the words I have written a great multitude: the presence of Zen Master Thich Nhat Hanh and his monastics and the deep mysticism of my own spiritual tradition. I see my parents, siblings, and friends; the great wisdom, love, and compassion of my wife, Paz; and the deep and spacious love I have for my two sons, Joseph and Isaac.

I would like also to express my appreciation to the whole team at Parallax Press for their hard and loving work to bring this book into existence and to the generosity and kindness of the team who work with Brother Phap Huu and me on *The Way Out Is In* podcast, which has been a catalyst for writing this book.

My father was a great teacher. He once wrote in a letter that living a true life was not about being handed a fragrant and beautiful rose, but was more akin to unpeeling an onion, layer by layer, with all the tears that come along with that process. While I am able to pay homage to the feelings of joy and ease that I have hopefully woven into the tapestry of this book, I also want to share appreciation for all the suffering and pain that has run like a river through my life, knowing that all the difficulties I have faced have been the grit needed to produce any pearls of wisdom you may have come across in this book.

References

Nhat Hanh, Thich. *The Heart of the Buddha's Teaching: Transforming Suffering into Peace, Joy, and Liberation.* New York: Harmony, 1999.

———. *The Mindfulness Survival Kit.* Berkeley, CA: Parallax Press, 2013.

———. *The Miracle of Mindfulness: An Introduction to the Practice of Meditation.* Boston, MA: Beacon Press, 1999.

———. *Old Path White Clouds: Walking in the Footsteps of the Buddha.* Berkeley, CA: Parallax Press, 1991.

———. *Work: How to Find Joy and Meaning in Each Hour of the Day.* Berkeley, CA: Parallax Press, 2012.

———. *Zen and the Art of Saving the Planet.* New York: HarperOne, 2021.

Sister Chan Khong. *Beginning Anew: Four Steps to Restoring Communication.* Berkeley, CA: Parallax Press, 2014.

Find guided Total Relaxation meditations on the Plum Village app, *plumvillage.app*.

For a video on the practice of Beginning Anew, visit *https://plumvillage.org/articles/begin-anew.*

About the Authors

BROTHER CHAN PHAP HUU (DHARMA NAME: DHARMA FRIEND) first encountered Zen Master Thich Nhat Hanh and the Plum Village community as a nine-year-old child when he traveled from Canada with his father and sister to Plum Village France in 1996. He was immediately drawn by the joyous brotherhood and the peaceful comportment of the monks. At the age of twelve, he knew that he wished to become a monk.

After much persistence on his part, his family allowed him to realize this wish at the age of thirteen. Brother Phap Huu was ordained as a novice monk in 2002. He received full bhikkhu ordination on December 18, 2006, and the Lamp Transmission as a Dharma Teacher in 2009. He became vice abbot in 2008 and has been the abbot of Upper Hamlet in January 2011, at the age of twenty-three.

True to his name, Brother Phap Huu became a dear friend to Thay. He was often by Thay's side as an attendant, sharing moments filled with love, laughter, tears, and inspiration. As an abbot, Brother Phap Huu takes time to connect with and understand his monastic and lay brothers and he is much appreciated as a skillful facilitator of gatherings. He is interested in team building, coaching, and mentoring, and he also loves basketball and music.

JO CONFINO (DHARMA NAME: SPIRITUAL FRIEND OF THE HEART) is an executive coach, spiritual mentor, workshop and retreat facilitator, journalist, and sustainability expert. He works at the intersection of personal transformation and systems change with several organizations, including Leaders' Quest and Global Optimism. Besides chairing and facilitating large-scale events and conferences all over the world for the past twenty years, he also runs workshops and roundtables. Jo has been supporting Plum Village for the past eighteen years and had the privilege to interview Zen Master Thich Nhat Hanh on many occasions.

Jo was an executive editor at *The Guardian* and chairman and editorial director of the Guardian Sustainable Business website. During his twenty-three years there, he helped create the *Guardian*'s environment and global development websites, as well as running "Living Our Values," a multi-year project to ensure the media organization was walking its talk. Before moving to live next door to Plum Village in 2020, he was executive editor, Impact and Innovation, and editorial director of "What's Working" at the HuffPost in New York. During his five years there, he developed long-term editorial projects based on social, environmental, and economic justice and was a member of the HuffPost senior leadership team as well as the senior leadership team of Verizon Media. Jo gained his MSc in Responsibility and Business Practice at the University of Bath.

About *The Way Out Is In* Podcast

Thich Nhat Hanh's calligraphy "The Way Out Is In" highlights that the way out of any difficulty is to look deeply within, gain insights, and then put them into practice.

This podcast series is aimed at helping us to transcend our fear and anger so that we can be more engaged in the world in a way that develops love and compassion.

The Way Out is In podcast is cohosted by Brother Phap Huu and Jo Confino and coproduced by the Plum Village App and Global Optimism, with support from the Thich Nhat Hanh Foundation, *tnhf.org*. You can listen to episodes on Spotify, Apple Podcasts, the Plum Village website *plumvillage.org*, and the Plum Village App *plumvillage.app*.

Monastics and visitors practice the art of mindful living in the tradition of Thich Nhat Hanh at our mindfulness practice centers around the world. To reach any of these communities, or for information about how individuals, couples, and families can join in a retreat, please contact:

PLUM VILLAGE
24240 Thénac, France
plumvillage.org

LA MAISON DE L'INSPIR
77510 Villeneuve-sur-Bellot, France
maisondelinspir.org

HEALING SPRING
MONASTERY
77510 Verdelot, France
healingspringmonastery.org

MAGNOLIA GROVE
MONASTERY
Batesville, MS 38606, USA
magnoliagrovemonastery.org

BLUE CLIFF MONASTERY
Pine Bush, NY 12566, USA
bluecliffmonastery.org

DEER PARK MONASTERY
Escondido, CA 92026, USA
deerparkmonastery.org

EUROPEAN INSTITUTE OF
APPLIED BUDDHISM
D-51545 Waldbröl, Germany
eiab.eu

THAILAND PLUM VILLAGE
*Nakhon Ratchasima
30130 Thailand*
thaiplumvillage.org

ASIAN INSTITUTE OF
APPLIED BUDDHISM
Lantau Island, Hong Kong
pvfhk.org

STREAM ENTERING
MONASTERY
Porcupine Ridge, Victoria 3461 Australia
nhapluu.org

MOUNTAIN SPRING
MONASTERY
Bilpin, NSW 2758, Australia
mountainspringmonastery.org

For more information visit: *plumvillage.org*
To find an online sangha visit: *plumline.org*
For more resources, try the Plum Village app: *plumvillage.app*
Social media: *@thichnhathanh @plumvillagefrance*

PARALLAX PRESS, a nonprofit publisher founded by Zen Master Thich Nhat Hanh, publishes books and media on the art of mindful living and Engaged Buddhism. We are committed to offering teachings that help transform suffering and injustice. Our aspiration is to contribute to collective insight and awakening, bringing about a more joyful, healthy, and compassionate society.

View our entire library at parallax.org.

THE MINDFULNESS BELL is a journal of the art of mindful living in the Plum Village tradition of Thich Nhat Hanh. To subscribe or to see the worldwide directory of Sanghas (local mindfulness groups), visit mindfulnessbell.org.